THE SCRIPTURES TESTIFY ABOUT ME

THE SCRIPTURES TESTIFY ABOUT ME

JESUS AND THE GOSPEL
IN THE
OLD TESTAMENT

EDITED BY D. A. CARSON

CROSSWAY

WHEATON, ILLINOIS

Library of Congress Cataloging-in-Publication Data

Gospel Coalition. National Conference (2011: Chicago, Ill.)
    The Scriptures testify about me: Jesus and the Gospel in the Old Testament / edited by D. A. Carson.
        pages cm
    Includes bibliographical references and indexes.
    ISBN 978-1-4335-3808-7 (tp)
    1. Typology (Theology)—Congresses. 2. Bible. O.T.—Criticism, interpretation, etc.—Congresses. 3. Bible. N.T.—Relation to the Old Testament—Congresses. 4. Jesus Christ—Person and offices—Biblical teaching—Congresses. I. Carson, D. A. II. Mohler, R. Albert, Jr., 1959– Studying the Scriptures and finding Jesus (John 5:31–47) III. Title.
BT225.G67 2011
232'.12—dc23   2012043961

CONTENTS

THE SCRIPTURES TESTIFY ABOUT ME

PREFACE

The book you hold in your hands contains the written form of the plenary addresses given in April 2011 at the national conference of The Gospel Coalition, in Chicago. The audio and video forms of those addresses are still available on our website (thegospel coalition.org).

The theme of that conference was "They Testify about Me: Preaching Jesus and the Gospel from the Old Testament." Not a few of the accompanying workshops were tied, directly or indirectly, to the same theme. The conference title has been slightly modified to become the title of this book.

So as not to arouse false expectations, I should specify what these eight plenary addresses do *not* provide. They do not provide a "how to" resource for preachers: a manual on "how to read the Old Testament in the light of the New," or something of that sort. The best "how to manual" along those lines is the book by G. K. Beale, *Handbook on the New Testament Use of the Old Testament: Exegesis and Interpretation.* Still less does the book you are reading attempt to comment on every place where the New Testament quotes or alludes to the Old: that would require a very large tome, and one is already available: G. K. Beale and D. A. Carson, eds., *Commentary on the New Testament Use of the Old Testament*, which is meant to be a reference tool for preachers and other Bible teachers.

What the addresses in this book offer is something more modest but with more immediate effect, namely, some examples of Christian preachers handling a variety of highly diverse Old Testament texts. The exception is the first chapter, which ably introduces the subject. The remaining seven focus squarely on Old Testament passages and bring the reader to Jesus and the gospel.

These seven expositions of Old Testament texts vary enormously as to how the Old Testament text is handled. In some cases the preacher focuses on the details of the text, and, because the text is demonstrably predictive, finds his way to Jesus in a straightforward fashion. In other cases the preacher relies on typology—on discerning the persons, places, and institutions that constitute massive patterns in the Old Testament that spin out into trajectories pointing forward to Jesus. In one or two cases, the preacher expounds the "big idea" of the assigned text and, in a kind of analogical argument, arrives at the same "big idea" in the person and work of Jesus Christ. Again, a preacher may show how the sequence of developing revelation in the Old Testament forces the reader toward the culmination of that sequence, Jesus himself.

In every case, our hope and prayer is that these expositions will prove not only clarifying but humbling, enriching, and edifying, as well as incentives to keep preaching and teaching Old Testament texts.

D. A. Carson

1

STUDYING THE SCRIPTURES AND FINDING JESUS

John 5:31–47

R. Albert Mohler Jr.

Meditating on the theme of preaching Jesus and the gospel from the Old Testament ought to thrill us. Some people might hear a theme like this and be puzzled by it, wondering what in the world we are even talking about. If we who are pastors are honest, however, we should be chastened that far too many members of our own churches might also wonder what we are talking about.

We think about these theological concerns with a sense of urgency and hope, even as we recognize that something has gone wrong. In his book *Generation Ex-Christian*, Drew Dyck writes of "leavers," his term for young people who have left evangelical churches.[1] Dyck provides a helpful typology of this group:

- Postmoderns think the evangelical message is too narrow.
- Recoilers had some bad church experiences and thus have written off the church.
- Modernists bought into an anti-supernatural worldview and now want nothing to do with biblical truth.
- Neo-pagans play around with various sorts of spirituality.
- Spiritual rebels insist on their own autonomy.
- Drifters wandered slowly away from the church.

[1] Drew Dyck, *Generation Ex-Christian: Why Young Adults Are Leaving the Faith . . . and How to Bring Them Back* (Chicago: Moody, 2010).

Although the church has always had those who have simply disappeared from us, evangelicals in our day recognize that a frighteningly large number of young people are leaving. This should cause us to ask some important questions. The most important and fundamental question is *why?*

In two recent books, Christian Smith and his team have described the spirituality of young people in America.[2] In their first study, they engage in a massive research project on what these young people actually believe. They define this belief system in terms of three words that should now be classic in our imagination: "moralistic therapeutic deism." These young people believe that God wants his creatures to behave, that God wants his creatures to feel good about themselves, and that God exists but is not involved in individual lives. Then, in the second work, Smith and his colleagues look at a large sample and focus on evangelicals who are now young adults—"emerging adults."

Kenda Creasy Dean, doing further research out of this same project, suggests in *Almost Christian* that many of these young people are not really Christian at all—at least not by any normal biblical, theological definition.[3] They are "Christian-ish."[4] Dean provides a severe indictment that almost certainly applies to more than just the younger generation in the United States. No wonder they leave—what is to keep them? We wonder how this happened. How did we as evangelicals do this to ourselves?

Looking closely at what these young people believe, one discovers that they have evidently never been taught the gospel of Jesus Christ. The absence of biblical, gospel preaching explains how we have created in our churches a generation of moralizing, therapeutic, practical deists.

We also minister within a context of very real challenges from

---

[2] Christian Smith, *Soul Searching: The Religious and Spiritual Lives of American Teenagers* (Oxford: Oxford University Press, 2005); Smith, *Souls in Transition: The Religious and Spiritual Lives of Emerging Adults* (Oxford: Oxford University Press, 2009).
[3] Kenda Creasy Dean, *Almost Christian: What the Faith of Our Teenagers Is Telling the American Church* (Oxford: Oxford University Press, 2010).
[4] Ibid. "Becoming Christian-ish" is the title of chapter 1.

Protestant liberalism. Although now nearly two centuries old, liberalism is back—it just returns again and again. There are open denials of inerrancy and open refutations of essential doctrines—even the metanarrative of the gospel is being rejected. There is a call for a new kind of Christianity, one that does not move from creation to fall to redemption and to consummation. That story is supposedly captive to Greco-Roman philosophy and not to Scripture. But in order to change the metanarrative, one has to deny a great deal of Scripture. Hence, the great relevance and urgency in thinking about the metanarrative of Scripture and the manner in which we preach the gospel of Jesus Christ from the Old Testament texts.

And yet, even with all these challenges, there is much to encourage us. In my travels, I have the privilege of meeting with people from all different generations and locations who are passionately committed to the gospel. And, when I am among the younger generation in particular, I meet with many who are confessional and convictional. They represent a wave of energy for planting gospel churches, as well as for reforming and recovering congregations. This is a missional generation driven by missiological vision. So there is a real reason for hope and a genuine reason for encouragement.

As we consider the theme of preaching Jesus and the gospel from the Old Testament, we turn to John 5:31–47 and find a powerful text wherein Jesus spoke of witnesses to his ministry:

If I alone bear witness about myself, my testimony is not true. There is another who bears witness about me, and I know that the testimony that he bears about me is true. You sent to John, and he has borne witness to the truth. Not that the testimony that I receive is from man, but I say these things so that you may be saved. He was a burning and shining lamp, and you were willing to rejoice for a while in his light. But the testimony that I have is greater than that of John. For the works that the Father has given me to accomplish, the very works that I am doing, bear witness about me that the Father has sent me. And the Fa-

ther who sent me has himself borne witness about me. His voice
you have never heard, his form you have never seen, and you
do not have his word abiding in you, for you do not believe the
one whom he has sent. You search the Scriptures because you
think that in them you have eternal life; and it is they that bear
witness about me, yet you refuse to come to me that you may
have life. I do not receive glory from people. But I know that
you do not have the love of God within you. I have come in my
Father's name, and you do not receive me. If another comes in
his own name, you will receive him. How can you believe, when
you receive glory from one another and do not seek the glory that
comes from the only God? Do not think that I will accuse you to
the Father. There is one who accuses you: Moses, on whom you
have set your hope. For if you believed Moses, you would believe
me; for he wrote of me. But if you do not believe his writings,
how will you believe my words?[5]

The background of this text is the christological declaration
and revelation that have already taken place in John 5. This chapter begins with the healing of the man at the pool of Bethesda.
Jesus asked the man, "Do you want to be healed?" (v. 6). He commanded, "Get up, take up your bed, and walk" (v. 8). "And at once
the man was healed" (v. 9). Then after demonstrating his own authority, Jesus declared:

Truly, truly, I say to you, the Son can do nothing of his own ac-
cord, but only what he sees the Father doing. For whatever the
Father does, that the Son does likewise. For the Father loves the
Son and shows him all that he himself is doing. And greater
works than these will he show him, so that you may marvel. For
as the Father raises the dead and gives them life, so also the
Son gives life to whom he will. The Father judges no one, but
has given all judgment to the Son, that all may honor the Son,
just as they honor the Father. Whoever does not honor the Son
does not honor the Father who sent him. Truly, truly, I say to
you, whoever hears my word and believes him who sent me has

[5] All Scripture quotations in this chapter are from the English Standard Version.

eternal life. He does not come into judgment, but has passed from death to life.

Truly, truly, I say to you, an hour is coming, and is now here, when the dead will hear the voice of the Son of God, and those who hear will live. For as the Father has life in himself, so he has granted the Son also to have life in himself. And he has given him authority to execute judgment, because he is the Son of Man. Do not marvel at this, for an hour is coming when all who are in the tombs will hear his voice and come out, those who have done good to the resurrection of life, and those who have done evil to the resurrection of judgment. (John 5:19–29)

The crucial issue of hearing and believing is essential to this text. Jesus offered a straightforward promise: "Whoever hears my word and believes him who sent me has eternal life" (v. 24). Those who hear will live, and there will be a day when even the dead will hear the voice of the Son of God. Hearing and believing lead to eternal life.

Jesus spoke about witnesses to his ministry. He acknowledged the necessity of witnesses, a reality that the Old Testament confirms (vv. 31–32). His ministry must be attested. A prophet's word must be tested; there must be witnesses.

For those who refuse to believe and receive him, Jesus set out witnesses. Like an attorney setting forth his case, Jesus brought forth four witnesses to make clear that he is not without adequate witnesses. The people simply refused to see what was put before them. They refused to hear the very witnesses whom the Father sent.

WITNESS 1: JOHN THE BAPTIST

Jesus described John the Baptist as "a burning and shining lamp" (John 5:35). Jesus spoke of John the Baptist in the most positive terms. Not only did the people hear John the Baptist; they sent for him (v. 33). They wanted to hear from him. They demanded to hear from him, and he bore "witness to the truth" (v. 33). Jesus did not receive his self-identity from John (v. 34), but John represented the gift of the Father to the people so they would know the identity of the Son.

The prologue to John's Gospel says that John "came as a witness, to bear witness about the light, that all might believe through him. He was not the light, but came to bear witness about the light. The true light, which gives light to everyone, was coming into the world" (1:7–9). The background of this is almost assuredly Psalm 132:13–17:

> For the LORD has chosen Zion;
>   he has desired it for his dwelling place:
> "This is my resting place forever;
>   here I will dwell, for I have desired it.
> I will abundantly bless her provisions;
>   I will satisfy her poor with bread.
> Her priests I will clothe with salvation,
>   and her saints will shout for joy.
> There I will make a horn to sprout for David;
>   I have prepared a lamp for my anointed."

Jesus was saying that the Father prepared the "lamp." The people saw the "lamp." They sought him out and even enjoyed him for a moment. But they did not receive his witness. Even as the Scriptures explained his role, the people refused to understand. They should have been expecting the one who was not the light, but would point to the light—the true light that saves. Jesus pointed to John the Baptist, the burning and shining light, and said, in effect: "He was ignited. The Father ignited John to give off the light to announce the coming of the Son of Man. But you would not see it."

There is a necessary Old Testament background to understanding John as witness. But the very people who should have recognized John the Baptist as the lamp prepared for God's anointed failed to recognize him. Jesus made clear that John's witness was for the benefit of the people. Yet sadly, when the witness testified, they would not receive his testimony.

But John the Baptist was not the only witness.

WITNESS 2: JESUS'S WORKS

Jesus's own works—the miracles, the signs—testified of him. His own works were, in effect, witnesses. Jesus performed these signs right before the eyes of those who said, "Give us a sign." But, they refused to see the signs for what they were. These acts and signs were intended to underline and reveal Christ's identity and thus his authority to authenticate his message. They were to bear witness that Jesus is the Christ, the very Son of God, the Davidic king, the Lord's anointed. But the people would not hear.

In the next chapter, John reports a miracle that is one of the first miracles many of us remember hearing about: the feeding of the five thousand (John 6:1–15). This miracle illustrates what Jesus said (John 5) about his works. After Jesus fed the five thousand, those who came to find Jesus asked him, "Then what sign do you do, that we may see and believe you? What work do you perform?" (John 6:30). Do not miss the audacity of their questions. They asked Jesus these questions the day *after* the feeding of the five thousand—*after* that miracle, *after* that sign, *after* that work. They refused to see it. They asked Jesus what sign he would give and what work he would perform, as if nothing had happened. They asked the question as if Jesus had not healed a man at the pool of Bethesda—a miracle about which they complained because Jesus did it on the Sabbath—and then miraculously fed the multitudes.

Jesus said, ". . . the very works that I am doing, bear witness about me" (John 5:36). But the works of Jesus were not the final witness.

WITNESS 3: THE FATHER

"The Father who sent me has himself borne witness about me. His voice you have never heard, his form you have never seen, and you do not have his word abiding in you, for you do not believe the one whom he has sent" (John 5:37–38). Here is one of the most stark and direct indictments from the mouth of Jesus. He told them that they did not have God's Word in them—that they had actually never heard.

Contrast that with Deuteronomy 4, where Moses reminded the children of Israel that they had not seen the Lord but had heard his voice. God's people *hear* God's voice. Has any other people heard the voice of God speaking in the midst of the fire and survived (cf. Deut. 5:26)? But now Jesus said, "You have actually *never* heard." They would not even hear when the Father spoke at Jesus's baptism, "This is my beloved Son with whom I am well pleased."

The first witness was John the Baptist, a burning and shining light; second were the works of Jesus himself; third was the Father's witness; and the fourth witness, climactically in Jesus's progression of argument, is the Scriptures.

WITNESS 4: THE SCRIPTURES

The text is hauntingly clear: "You search the Scriptures because you think that in them you have eternal life; and it is they that bear witness about me, yet you refuse to come to me that you may have life" (John 5:39–40).

"You search the Scriptures" describes a very good thing. Jesus certainly does not counsel people *not* to search the Scriptures. Searching the Scriptures is what believers do. It is what we are taught to do. It is what we rightly do. But what is so horrible and humbling is that people can devote their lives to searching the Scriptures yet miss the point—and not be saved.

The entire Scriptures—and Jesus was referring specifically to the Old Testament—bear witness to Jesus. In other words, Jesus said, in effect, "You cannot read those words without reading of me. You cannot read the Law without reading of me. You cannot read the History without reading of me. You cannot read the Psalms without reading of me. You cannot read the Prophets without reading of me."

"It is they that bear witness about me." The climactic, confirming, final witness is Scripture. Therefore, a people trained in the

Scriptures should have been ready for Christ. They should have been anticipating him. They should have been looking and yearning for him. They should have been ready for his coming because the Old Testament constantly, continually, cumulatively, and consistently testifies to Christ.

We do not look to the Old Testament merely to find the *background* for Christ and his ministry, nor even for references that anticipate him. We must find Christ in the Old Testament—not here and there but everywhere. Christ validated the serious study of searching the Scriptures, but he warned that the most serious student of the Scriptures could miss the entire point. Jesus was not speaking to Scripture illiterates or to people who lacked serious study of the Scriptures. He was not speaking to those who refused to devote themselves to biblical scholarship. He was not speaking to those who took the Scriptures frivolously. Rather, he was speaking to those who had devoted their entire lives to studying the Scriptures, but missed the entire point.

Note that Jesus did not say that this "missing the point" was an intellectual problem. It was not a lack of knowledge. Their problem was moral, theological, and spiritual. The people refused to see:

- "You refuse to come to me" (John 5:40).
- "You do not receive me" (v. 43).
- "You . . . do not seek the glory that comes from the only God" (v. 44).

Jesus indicted them.

Jesus then cited Moses as their accuser. The very one they cited as their authority accused them. Jesus described Moses as the one "on whom you have set your hope" (v. 45), but Moses had set his hope upon Jesus. And "if you do not believe his writings, how will you believe my words?" (v. 47). In other words, Jesus accused them of refusing to hear what Jesus was telling them. Jesus indicted them for their absolute refusal to hear and believe what the Scriptures had taught them.

When Jesus spoke of these four witnesses, it was not that they were lacking or hidden. They were right before the people. The witnesses came and testified, but the people would not see, hear, and believe.

After Jesus healed the man who was blind from birth, the Pharisees accused the man during his second interrogation: "You are [Jesus's] disciple, but we are disciples of Moses. We know that God has spoken to Moses, but as for this man, we do not know where he comes from" (John 9:28–29). Again, they validated exactly what Jesus said about them in John 5. In other words, "You think that you have set your hope upon Moses, but Moses set his hope upon me. Moses wrote about me. You claim to be the sons of Moses, but you betray that you are not when you say, 'but as for this man, we do not know where he comes from.'" They betrayed not ignorance but willful rejection, willful blindness, and willful deafness.

We often hear people speak of New Testament Christianity, and we understand what they mean. But make no mistake, we are called to *biblical* Christianity. Christ himself declares that there is *Old Testament* Christianity. The Old Testament includes the gospel. Jesus is present in the Old Testament, not merely when speaking of Moses in a text like the following: "I will raise up for them a prophet like you from among their brothers. And I will put my words in his mouth, and he shall speak to them all that I command him" (Deut. 18:18); but also in all that Moses wrote and in all that the prophets have said. Jesus is present in all the Scriptures.

IDEOLOGICAL AND THEOLOGICAL DISMISSALS OF THE OLD TESTAMENT

Throughout the Gospel of John, Jesus rebuked those who should know, who should see, who should hear, who should believe—and yet, will not. Jesus indicted the people who claimed to be not just the sons of Moses, but also the sons of Abraham—yet would not hear, believe, and be saved.

The Jews said to him, . . . "Are you greater than our father Abraham, who died? And the prophets died! Who do you make yourself out to be?" Jesus answered, "If I glorify myself, my glory is nothing. It is my Father who glorifies me, of whom you say, 'He is our God.' But you have not known him [cf. John 5:37: "His voice you have never heard"]. I know him. If I were to say that I do not know him, I would be a liar like you, but I do know him and I keep his word. Your father Abraham rejoiced that he would see my day. He saw it and was glad." So the Jews said to him, "You are not yet fifty years old, and have you seen Abraham?" Jesus said to them, "Truly, truly, I say to you, before Abraham was, I am." (John 8:52–58)

But these words also rebuke the church of the Lord Jesus Christ in our own generation for our misuse and neglect of the Old Testament. In our own way, we can commit the same insult to both Christ and the Scriptures. For many, the Old Testament is simply a problem. Throughout the history of the Christian church, there have been those who have struggled to understand what to do with the Old Testament. Some of the sources of the problem are ideological and theological.

First, in a context of political correctness—particularly within the academy—some call the Old Testament the "Hebrew Scriptures" or the "Hebrew Bible." Unless that designation does no more than highlight the dominant language, a Christian cannot accept the term because it insinuates that the Old Testament is someone else's book, that it is foreign territory to the church.

Second, there is the historical Marcionite impulse to reject the Old Testament as revealing a different deity. It is frightening to see how many evangelical children and young people just assume that this is indeed the pattern. They pick it up one way or the other and are little Marcionites. You wonder where they get this idea, and then you talk to their parents. There are Marcionites in our pews and in far too many of our pulpits. Many of them do not know it. They are *practical* Marcionites, even if not card-carrying ones.

Third, some argue that the Old Testament should be read only on its own terms without any reference to the New Testament. Some suggest this even within the Christian church, even within some evangelical institutions and faculties. It comes down to insisting that Christians need to do synagogue readings when we come to the Old Testament.

Fourth, classical dispensationalism is right to see ethical development but wrong to deny continuity. Taken at face value, the classical dispensationalists argued for what amounted to two completely different ethical systems in the two Testaments. They were certainly right to point to the higher law found in the New Testament, but wrong to argue against the basic continuity of the covenants, with the Old Testament and the law completely fulfilled in the person and work of Christ. This exegetical and theological error has opened the door to much mischief and misunderstanding.

Fifth, there is a moral argument against the Old Testament, an updated Marcionite temptation. It is not particularly new, but it became more focused in the twentieth and twenty-first centuries. In his Lyman Beecher lectures on preaching, given at Yale in the early part of the twentieth century, Harry Emerson Fosdick spoke of the task of preaching the Old Testament in general, and a very specific text in particular, as "intellectually ruinous and morally debilitating."[6] Fosdick said that modern people rightly recoil from these Old Testament texts, and that it would be an insult to modern morality to try to preach them or even to try to rescue them in some way. Fosdick said we should not try to harmonize them or come to terms with them. Rather, we should just write off sections of the biblical text as the musings of an ancient nomadic people and be done with it.

More recently, Kenton Sparks, in his denial of biblical inerrancy, wrote of the Old Testament and "biblical texts that strike us as downright sinister or evil."[7] In like manner, Brian McLaren

---

[6] Harry Emerson Fosdick, *The Modern Use of the Bible* (New York: Macmillan, 1924), 27.
[7] Kenton L. Sparks, "After Inerrancy: Evangelicals and the Bible in a Postmodern Age, Part 2," The BioLogos Forum: Science and Faith in Dialogue, June 10, 2010, accessed http://biologos.org/blog /after-inerrancy-evangelicals-and-the-bible-in-a-postmodern-age-part-2. Cf. Kenton L. Sparks,

wrote about the Genesis account of God's actions in the story of Noah and described the story as "profoundly disturbing."[8]

IGNORANCE AND NEGLECT OF THE OLD TESTAMENT

But these ideological and theological dismissals of the Old Testament are not the main problem in our midst. In our circles—our pulpits, Sunday school classes, and Bible study groups—the biggest problem is the ignorance and neglect of the Old Testament. We must admit it: a good many evangelical preachers and Bible teachers simply have no idea what to do with the Old Testament.

Few remember Leslie Poles Hartley's 1953 novel *The Go-Between*, and most people tend to remember only the opening line: "The past is a foreign country: they do things differently there." To many Christians and even pastors and preachers, the Old Testament is a foreign book. They do things differently there. And they certainly do: arks and animals in a menagerie afloat, dead animals and hewn bullocks, rams in thickets, slavery in Egypt, burning bushes, staffs that turn into snakes, bronze serpents, manna in the morning, pillars of fire and columns of smoke, convoluted history of conquests of kings, intrigue, adultery, murder, incest, a preoccupation with bodily fluids, bears who eat boys, boys who kill giants, prophets who taunt idolaters, prophets who throw fits, prophets who sit by gates and weep, poetry that reads like praise, poetry that reads like existentialist philosophy, Persian writing on walls, foreign kings who roam like wild beasts, a prostitute who hides spies, spies who lose heart, women who summon courage, donkeys that talk, a strong man who commits suicide, stuttering leaders, naked patriarchs, majestic praise, predictive prophecy, lamentation, law, statutes, ordinances—in all of its glory. And all of it reveals Christ. Every bit of it.

They do things differently there, and that is the point. These

---

God's Word in Human Words: An Evangelical Appropriation of Critical Biblical Scholarship (Grand Rapids: Baker, 2008).

[8] Brian D. McLaren, *A New Kind of Christianity: Ten Questions That Are Transforming the Faith* (New York: HarperOne, 2010), 108.

things all anticipate Christ. They look forward to Christ and make us yearn for Christ. They should help us to recognize the Christ. "It is they that bear witness about me" (John 5:39).

HOW EVANGELICAL PREACHERS MISUSE THE OLD TESTAMENT

In what ways do evangelical preachers misuse the Old Testament?

First, many preachers simply avoid the Old Testament at all costs. I have actually heard some preachers state as a matter of principle that they preach from the New Testament because it is the Christian book. They are practical Marcionites. They are robbing their people of the knowledge of Christ from the Scriptures. How impoverished is that preaching and how undernourished are those congregations. Speaking of the Old Testament, Fosdick said, "All the king's horses and all the king's men could hardly drag them [i.e., preachers] into dealing with certain [Old Testament] passages that used to be the glory of our fathers' preaching."[9]

Second, many evangelical preachers actually teach Old Testament texts and say a few words about them, but mostly as background—as though the Old Testament were a different story before we get to "our" story, the real story. But Christ says in John 5 (and the rest of the New Testament agrees) that it is all one story. The Old Testament is not the story we have to know before we know the real story. Rather, the gospel is in all of it.

Third, preachers moralize the Old Testament. We know we ought not to do that, but it is second nature to us. God made us moral creatures. We moralize even when we do not want to do so. We moralize about moralizing. Of course, apart from the gospel of Jesus Christ, the only alternative to a moralizing creature is a sociopath.

The problem starts very early. We are raised to hear the Scripture, especially the Old Testament, in moralizing terms. That is how we are taught from the very beginning. Look at the Bible story

---

[9] Fosdick, *The Modern Use of the Bible*, 1.

books for children. Most of them (not all of them, thanks be to God) are dripping with morality tales. It is as if the Old Testament is our Jewish-Christian form of Aesop's Fables: do this; do not do that. It starts at the parent's knee, and then continues in Sunday school and Vacation Bible School—all the children's church programs ratify it. We have updated our pedagogical technology from flannelgraphs to PowerPoint, but it is still moralizing.

So, when we arrive at the period of adolescence that Christian Smith and his colleagues studied, we discover that the basic belief system of most of our adolescents is moralistic therapeutic deism. Well, that is what they received from us, and not just from our preaching of the Old Testament; moralizing is what they heard from virtually all our preaching. In fact, if there is any period of life that tends to be subjected to moralizing in the most eccentric and intensive ways, it is adolescence. That is what most Christian youth ministries do. From generation to generation, they just update and add new subjects to the moralizing of adolescents.

But moralizing is not what our text is about. More precisely, moralizing is not the redemptive purpose of the text. That is not how it testifies of Christ. There are moral lessons there, and we are wrong to ignore them. Even the New Testament sometimes cites the Old Testament in terms of moral lessons we should learn. When it does, we must learn them. But it is wrong to think that moralizing is the main point of the New Testament's use of the Old. It is tragic to make moralizing the main thing.

Those whom Jesus rebuked in John 5 would agree with every moralistic point that any Christian preacher makes and probably a great deal more that we would not even think to make. It is not wrong to see David as a boy who demonstrated courage because of his faith in God; David killed the giant when others cowered. The problem, however, is in missing the greater point. The redemptive content is that David was God's anointed, the king whose dynasty would never end. This content points directly to King Jesus, seated on David's throne—the one who is prophet, priest, and king.

Moralism is the default mode for preachers. It's second nature.

But it horribly misinforms the congregation. It horribly malforms their understanding of the gospel because it tells them what they really want to hear, which is that they can please God through moral improvement. But moralizing cannot save. We must do better than this if we are to escape the rebuke of Christ: "If you believed Moses, you would believe me" (John 5:46).

HOW CHRISTIANS THROUGHOUT CHURCH HISTORY HAVE INTERPRETED THE OLD TESTAMENT

The Church Fathers

The Old Testament has been a challenge in the history of the Christian church—not only in recent centuries but going all the way back to the early church. One of the ways that church fathers dealt with the Old Testament was to allegorize it—a literary and imaginative form of moralizing. They added a good deal to it that most of us would find not only antiquarian but also having little to do with the text. They knew they had to do something with the Old Testament, and there are some faithful examples even among the Patristic fathers. But it is clear that the Christian church was already struggling with what to do with the Old Testament.

Martin Luther

Fast-forward to the Reformation and one encounters Martin Luther, who saw in the Scriptures a radical dichotomy between law and gospel. Yet, Luther came to understand, along with the apostle Paul, that even though the law cannot save, there is grace in the law. Luther was not sure what to do with this. He was not even consistent with what to do with the law in his teaching and personal life. In his early ministry as a Reformer, Luther emphatically urged young preachers to avoid preaching the law. Then Luther had children. And note the content of the first section of his "Small Catechism," written for the training of children: "The Ten Commandments."[10] There is grace in that, too.

---

[10] Martin Luther, *Luther's Small Catechism* (Minneapolis: Augsburg, 2001).

John Calvin

John Calvin represents a fountain of health on this. His *Institutes of the Christian Religion* methodologically and theologically sets this out with grandeur. It is hard in our contemporary context to imagine better than what he teaches us. The title of book 2 of the *Institutes* is "Of the Knowledge of God the Redeemer, in Christ, as First Manifested to the Fathers, under the Law, and Thereafter to Us under the Gospel." Could any of us state it better than that?

The title of chapter 7 of book 2 is "The Law Given, Not to Retain a People for Itself, but to Keep Alive the Hope of Salvation in Christ until His Advent." So we see that the purpose of the law is to foster hope.

The title of chapter 9 of book 2 is "Christ, Though Known to the Jews under the Law, yet Manifested Only under the Gospel." It is not that we do not need the gospel. It is by the gospel that we are saved. But we should know our need for the gospel and the promise of the gospel, and the Christ promised us in the gospel, even by reading the law. As Paul wrote in Romans 7, without the law he would not have known that he was a coveter (v. 7). Until that knowledge came, he did not know that he needed a Savior. There is grace in the knowledge of our sin, and there is grace in our knowledge of the need for a Savior. And there is grace in the fact that a Savior was all along promised and revealed, even under the law.

In speaking of how we should be trained by the New Testament to read the Old Testament, Calvin pointed to 1 Peter 1:10–12:

> Concerning this salvation, the prophets who prophesied about the grace that was to be yours searched and inquired carefully, inquiring what person or time the Spirit of Christ in them was indicating when he predicted the sufferings of Christ and the subsequent glories. It was revealed to them that they were serving not themselves but you, in the things that have now been announced to you through those who preached the good news to you by the Holy Spirit sent from heaven, things into which angels long to look.

In our own day, how impoverished we would be if we did not have witnesses such as Geerhardus Vos, Richard Gaffin, Edmund Clowney, and others who taught not only a new generation but now also successive generations the importance of seeing a redemptive-historical hermeneutic and applying it to all the Scriptures. In recent years, there has been a renaissance, a recovery, and even a celebration of how to preach the Bible as a whole. We are rediscovering how to understand the metanarrative—to find great joy in preaching it and even greater joy in coming to see people understand it. I am so thankful for works by such influential figures as Graeme Goldsworthy, Sidney Greidanus, and Bryan Chapell— scholars who have literally changed categories for us.

HEBREWS

Even as Calvin argued from 1 Peter, we need to let the New Testament teach us how to read the Old Testament. As such, where better to look than the book of Hebrews? It begins by telling us, "Long ago, at many times and in many ways, God spoke to our fathers by the prophets, but in these last days he has spoken to us by his Son, whom he appointed the heir of all things, through whom also he created the world" (Heb. 1:1–2). This is the continuous pattern of divine revelation: all redemptive, all pointing to the climactic revelation in Christ.

What about Moses? Moses was the one, Jesus said, "on whom you have set your hope" (John 5:45). "Now Moses was faithful in all God's house as a servant, to testify to the things that were to be spoken later, but Christ is faithful over God's house as a son" (Heb. 3:5–6). We should greatly respect Moses. He was central, even essential, in the Old Testament. He played an important part in salvation history. But Moses was a "servant" in God's house; Christ is a "son."

What about Joshua? Or what about the Sabbath? "For if Joshua had given them rest, God would not have spoken of another day later on. So then, there remains a Sabbath rest for the people of

God, for whoever has entered God's rest has also rested from his works as God did from his" (Heb. 4:8–10). What should we have learned from the Sabbath as an institution or as a command? We should have learned that we must have an eternal Sabbath when we rest not only from our earthly labors but also from our attempts at self-righteousness to prove ourselves just before a holy God. Or, what about Abraham?

> For when God made a promise to Abraham, since he had no one greater by whom to swear, he swore by himself, saying, "Surely I will bless you and multiply you." And thus Abraham, having patiently waited, obtained the promise. For people swear by something greater than themselves, and in all their disputes an oath is final for confirmation. So when God desired to show more convincingly to the heirs of the promise the unchangeable character of his purpose, he guaranteed it with an oath, so that by two unchangeable things, in which it is impossible for God to lie, we who have fled for refuge might have strong encouragement to hold fast to the hope set before us. We have this as a sure and steadfast anchor of the soul, a hope that enters into the inner place behind the curtain, where Jesus has gone as a forerunner on our behalf, having become a high priest forever after the order of Melchizedek. (Heb. 6:13–20)

Or what should we have seen when we heard of Melchizedek? We should have seen that if Abraham gave an offering to Melchizedek, then there is something greater to which Melchizedek is pointing. And the author of Hebrews points us there:

> For it was indeed fitting that we should have such a high priest, holy, innocent, unstained, separated from sinners, and exalted above the heavens. He has no need, like those high priests, to offer sacrifices daily, first for his own sins and then for those of the people, since he did this once for all when he offered up himself. For the law appoints men in their weakness as high priests, but the word of the oath, which came later than the law, appoints a Son who has been made perfect forever. (Heb. 7:26–28)

We should have been looking for the Son.

> Now the point in what we are saying is this: we have such a high priest, one who is seated at the right hand of the throne of the Majesty in heaven, a minister in the holy places, in the true tent that the Lord set up, not man. For every high priest is appointed to offer gifts and sacrifices; thus it is necessary for this priest also to have something to offer. Now if he were on earth, he would not be a priest at all, since there are priests who offer gifts according to the law. They serve a copy and shadow of the heavenly things. For when Moses was about to erect the tent, he was instructed by God, saying, "See that you make everything according to the pattern that was shown you on the mountain." But as it is, Christ has obtained a ministry that is as much more excellent than the old as the covenant he mediates is better, since it is enacted on better promises. For if that first covenant had been faultless, there would have been no occasion to look for a second. (Heb. 8:1–7)

We should have been able to look to the tabernacle and see not only the Holy Place but also the Most Holy Place. Even the furnishings in the tabernacle point to Christ. And we should have been able to see what was going on in the tabernacle (and later in the temple) and say, "There has to be something that will eliminate this veil. Someone is going to have to do something to achieve peace with God. And, of course, God will have to do that thing." As he did in Christ:

> But when Christ appeared as a high priest of the good things that have come, then through the greater and more perfect tent (not made with hands, that is, not of this creation) he entered once for all into the holy places, not by means of the blood of goats and calves but by means of his own blood, thus securing an eternal redemption. For if the blood of goats and bulls, and the sprinkling of defiled persons with the ashes of a heifer, sanctify for the purification of the flesh, how much more will the blood of Christ, who through the eternal Spirit offered himself without blemish to God, purify our conscience from dead works to serve the living God. (Heb. 9:11–14)

Christ has appeared. He is the "high priest of the good things that have come." He entered the tabernacle not made with human hands. He entered it once for all time. In other words, in looking to the sacrificial system of old, we should have seen the succession of Levitical priests coming one after another, generation after generation, performing sacrifice after sacrifice. In so doing, we should have realized that this does not achieve eternal life. It does not eventuate in eternal life. It does not secure an eternal redemption.

In my own Pelagian stage (and this is where just about every adolescent is at some point), I had a hard time sleeping at night over the issue of confession of sin. I had come to recognize myself as a sinner, and this recognition, by God's grace, was stronger than I had ever had at any other point in my life. Scripture instructed me that sin was ever before me. So I would pray a prayer of confession and then think, "What if I die before I confess again? I am going to fall short of the glory of God before I get up off of my knees. I am a dead man."

In my own way, I was asking, "What's going to happen if the priests are not allowed into the temple? What is going to happen if the temple is no more?" But then we discover that Christ is our great high priest, and he accomplishes this by being the Mediator of a new covenant.

CONCLUSION

All of these things point to a fulfillment that only God in Christ can accomplish. We should have seen it. In Luke 24, as Jesus walked to Emmaus with the men, he rebuked them:

> And he said to them, "O foolish ones, and slow of heart to believe all that the prophets have spoken! Was it not necessary that the Christ should suffer these things and enter into his glory?" And beginning with Moses and all the Prophets, he interpreted to them in all the Scriptures the things concerning himself.
>
> So they drew near to the village to which they were going. He acted as if he were going farther, but they urged him strongly,

saying, "Stay with us, for it is toward evening and the day is now far spent." So he went in to stay with them. When he was at table with them, he took the bread and blessed and broke it and gave it to them. And their eyes were opened, and they recognized him. And he vanished from their sight. They said to each other, "Did not our hearts burn within us while he talked to us on the road, while he opened to us the Scriptures?" (Luke 24:25–32)

First the rebuke: "O foolish ones, and slow of heart to believe all that the prophets have spoken!" Then the cure: "And beginning with Moses and all the Prophets, he interpreted to them in all the Scriptures the things concerning himself." Then the blessing: "Did not our hearts burn within us while he talked to us on the road, while he opened to us the Scriptures?"

We must preach Christ from *all* the Scriptures and find Christ in the gospel of the Old Testament as well as in the New. We need to allow the New Testament to train us how to read the Old. We must put the Bible back into the hands of believers—intact and whole—with Christ and the gospel of our redemption at the center.

And we pray to see what Luke recounts for us; we pray to see it happen again and again. Preachers, we pray to see this happen every time the Word of God is preached. Church of the Lord Jesus Christ, we should pray for this to happen in our midst every time we open the Word. We should pray to see Christ's people ask, "Did not our hearts burn within us?"

All it takes is to open up the book.

GETTING OUT

Exodus 14

Tim Keller

I feel like an actor in a play who not only is part of the story on the stage but also occasionally turns aside and speaks directly to the audience. I want to preach Christ from the Old Testament to you, and I also want to teach you something about how to preach Christ from the Old Testament. I feel like I need both to preach to you and to give asides—"Now by the way, when you do that, do this." This is challenging, but it's also a great deal of fun.

Let's read the account of the climax of the exodus: the crossing of the Red Sea in Exodus 14:5-31:

> When the king of Egypt was told that the people had fled, Pharaoh and his officials changed their minds about them and said, "What have we done? We have let the Israelites go and have lost their services!" So he had his chariot made ready and took his army with him. He took six hundred of the best chariots, along with all the other chariots of Egypt, with officers over all of them. The LORD hardened the heart of Pharaoh king of Egypt, so that he pursued the Israelites, who were marching out boldly. The Egyptians—all Pharaoh's horses and chariots, horsemen and troops—pursued the Israelites and overtook them as they camped by the sea near Pi Hahiroth, opposite Baal Zephon.
>
> As Pharaoh approached, the Israelites looked up, and there were the Egyptians, marching after them. They were terrified and cried out to the LORD. They said to Moses, "Was it because there were no graves in Egypt that you brought us to the desert

to die? What have you done to us by bringing us out of Egypt? Didn't we say to you in Egypt, 'Leave us alone; let us serve the Egyptians'? It would have been better for us to serve the Egyptians than to die in the desert!"

Moses answered the people, "Do not be afraid. Stand firm and you will see the deliverance the LORD will bring you today. The Egyptians you see today you will never see again. The LORD will fight for you; you need only to be still."

Then the LORD said to Moses, "Why are you crying out to me? Tell the Israelites to move on. Raise your staff and stretch out your hand over the sea to divide the water so that the Israelites can go through the sea on dry ground. I will harden the hearts of the Egyptians so that they will go in after them. And I will gain glory through Pharaoh and all his army, through his chariots and his horsemen. The Egyptians will know that I am the LORD when I gain glory through Pharaoh, his chariots and his horsemen."

Then the angel of God, who had been traveling in front of Israel's army, withdrew and went behind them. The pillar of cloud also moved from in front and stood behind them, coming between the armies of Egypt and Israel. Throughout the night the cloud brought darkness to the one side and light to the other side; so neither went near the other all night long.

Then Moses stretched out his hand over the sea, and all that night the LORD drove the sea back with a strong east wind and turned it into dry land. The waters were divided, and the Israelites went through the sea on dry ground, with a wall of water on their right and on their left.

The Egyptians pursued them, and all Pharaoh's horses and chariots and horsemen followed them into the sea. During the last watch of the night the LORD looked down from the pillar of fire and cloud at the Egyptian army and threw it into confusion. He jammed the wheels of their chariots so that they had difficulty driving. And the Egyptians said, "Let's get away from the Israelites! The LORD is fighting for them against Egypt."

Then the LORD said to Moses, "Stretch out your hand over the sea so that the waters may flow back over the Egyptians and their chariots and horsemen." Moses stretched out his hand over the sea, and at daybreak the sea went back to its place. The Egyptians were fleeing toward it, and the LORD swept them into the sea. The water flowed back and covered the chariots and horsemen—the entire army of Pharaoh that had followed the Israelites into the sea. Not one of them survived. But the Israelites went through the sea on dry ground, with a wall of water on their right and on their left. That day the LORD saved Israel from the hands of the Egyptians, and Israel saw the Egyptians lying dead on the shore. And when the Israelites saw the mighty hand of the LORD displayed against the Egyptians, the people feared the LORD and put their trust in him and in Moses his servant.[1]

It is hard to overstate the importance of the Red Sea crossing for the rest of the Bible. There are about two dozen direct references to the Red Sea crossing in the rest of the Old Testament, and there are innumerable allusions to it. In the New Testament, there are significant statements like these:

1. "Out of Egypt I called my son" (Matt. 2:15). Matthew quotes Hosea 11:1, which refers to the exodus. The "son" in Hosea 11:1 is Israel, so Matthew directly connects Jesus's work and the exodus.
2. At Jesus's transfiguration, "Two men, Moses and Elijah, appeared in glorious splendor, talking with Jesus. They spoke about his departure [ἔξοδον], which he was about to bring to fulfillment at Jerusalem" (Luke 9:30–31). The word "departure" sounds like they are talking about Jesus's death, and they are. But the Greek word there is the word *exodos*, a big hint that Luke is saying that what Jesus accomplished in Jerusalem is the ultimate getting-out, the ultimate exodus.
3. Jesus is the greater Moses; Moses points to Jesus (Heb. 3:1–6).
4. "By faith the people passed through the Red Sea as on dry land; but when the Egyptians tried to do so, they were drowned" (Heb. 11:29). The Egyptians drowned because they didn't have faith. Hebrews 11 talks about *Christian* faith, and it uses the Red Sea crossing as a paradigm for Christian faith.

---

[1] All Scripture quotations in this chapter are from the New International Version.

5. "For I do not want you to be ignorant of the fact, brothers and sisters, that our ancestors were all under the cloud and that they all passed through the sea. They were all baptized into Moses in the cloud and in the sea. . . . Now these things occurred as examples to keep us [i.e., us Christians] from setting our hearts on evil things as they did" (1 Cor. 10:1–2, 6).

If there is one Old Testament passage that the New Testament invites us to read in a Christ-centered way as a paradigm of Christ's salvation, it's the exodus.

I'll never forget nearly forty years ago sitting in R. C. Sproul's living room in Stahlstown, Pennsylvania. Alec Motyer, a British Old Testament scholar I had never heard of, was visiting. I was on the floor with a bunch of other college and seminary students, and Sproul said to Motyer, "Tell us about the connection between the Old and New Testaments." Motyer replied something like this:

Think about it. Think of what an Israelite would say on the way to Canaan after passing through the Red Sea. If you asked an Israelite, "Who are you?" he might reply, "I was in a foreign land under the sentence of death and in bondage, but I took shelter under the blood of the lamb. And our mediator led us out, and we crossed over. Now we're on our way to the Promised Land, though we're not there yet. But he has given us his law to make us a community, and he has given us a tabernacle because we must live by grace and forgiveness. And he is present in our midst, and he will stay with us until we arrive home.

Then Motyer added, "That's exactly what a Christian says—almost word for word." And my twenty-three-year-old self thought, "Huh."

What can we learn from the Red Sea crossing about Jesus and our salvation? Three lessons: salvation is about getting out, but it's about

1. *what* we're getting out of: bondage with layers;
2. *how* we're getting out of it: crossing over by grace;
3. *why* we can get out of it: the Mediator.

That's how the story of the exodus connects with the rest of the Bible. We would not make these connections without the rest of the Bible, but the connections are clear when we look at the Bible's sweeping story line.

SALVATION IS ABOUT WHAT WE'RE GETTING OUT OF: BONDAGE WITH LAYERS

Salvation is about getting us out of bondage. That's what the word *redemption* means.

"When the king of Egypt was told that the people had fled, Pharaoh and his officials changed their minds about them and said, 'What have we done? We have let the Israelites go and have lost their services!'" (Ex. 14:5). "Services." What a nice way of putting it. Why didn't the Egyptians simply go out and *hire* someone else? No, they lost their entire *slave* labor force. The Israelites were slaves.

Pharaoh said, "We're gonna go get 'em. We let them go, but we've changed our minds. Let's go get 'em. We're gonna bring 'em back or kill 'em."

The old slave masters, who had released the Israelites, got in their chariots and chased down the Israelites. When the Israelites saw them coming,

> They were terrified and cried out to the LORD. They said to Moses, "Was it because there were no graves in Egypt that you brought us to the desert to die? What have you done to us by bringing us out of Egypt? Didn't we say to you in Egypt, 'Leave us alone; let us serve the Egyptians'? It would have been better for us to serve the Egyptians than to die in the desert!" (14:10–12)

The Israelites claimed that when Moses had said, "Let's go," they had replied, "It'd be better to stay. We like it here." But is that really what they'd said? Let's see:

> Moses and Aaron brought together all the elders of the Israelites, and Aaron told them everything the LORD had said to Moses. He

also performed the signs before the people, and they believed. And when they heard that the LORD was concerned about them and had seen their misery, they bowed down and worshiped. (Ex. 4:29–31)

That's not quite what the Israelites remembered. And this wasn't the last time the Israelites would do this.

In the desert the whole community grumbled against Moses and Aaron. The Israelites said to them, "If only we had died by the LORD's hand in Egypt! *There we sat around pots of meat and ate all the food we wanted,* but you have brought us out into this desert to starve this entire assembly to death." (Ex. 16:2–3)

There is no more basic word in the Bible than *redemption*. The Greek word for redemption means to loose. Redemption means to be released from bondage. The very heart of our understanding what salvation is all about is release from bondage.

The Israelites are a picture of us. They were in bondage. But this bondage had layers. The Israelites got out of bondage, but even though they were out of bondage, the slave masters said, "No, we want you back." Not only were the Israelites objectively free from bondage and yet now the slave masters wanted them back, but inside, subjectively in their hearts, they were not free from bondage. They still operated as slaves. You can take the people out of slavery, but you can't take the slavery out of the people as easily. Throughout the Bible, there are layers to the bondage from which God redeems his people. Here are four of them.

CHRISTIANS WERE OBJECTIVELY IN BONDAGE TO THE LAW BUT ARE NOW FREED FROM IT

We were objectively in bondage to the law. We were under guilt and condemnation. We have sinned. We do not love God with our whole being or love our neighbor as ourselves. We were under God's wrath, which is his settled, judicial opposition to evil and sin. God's wrath is objective, and our guilt is objective. We were in bondage to the law that brought condemnation. We were under the law.

But through Jesus we got out. "There is now no condemnation for those who are in Christ Jesus" (Rom. 8:1). "Sin shall no longer be your master, because you are not under the law, but under grace" (Rom. 6:14). That is objective freedom.

But there are more layers.

CHRISTIANS ARE SUBJECTIVELY IN BONDAGE TO THE LAW, AND THEY DEFAULT TO WORKS-RIGHTEOUSNESS

The whole book of Galatians is about people who, from what we can tell, were objectively freed from guilt (i.e., they seem to have really believed in Jesus), but were going back into a form of works-righteousness. Why? This is a bit of a speculation, but as a pastor over the years and as a human being, I think that deep down inside—maybe it's because of the image of God—everyone knows that he or she should be perfect. We all know that we should be perfect.

Parenting can affect this basic intuition. Some parents aggravate it by being very cruel, impossible to please, maybe abusive. Their kids grow up needing to prove themselves or hating themselves.

Another kind of bad parenting is self-esteem-ism. Parents tell their children over and over again, "You can do anything you want. You can be anyone you want." Right: "I'm twenty-three years old. I'm 5'3". I'm 123 pounds." "If you want to be an NFL linebacker, you just have to go for it with all you've got. You must climb every mountain, ford every stream, follow every rainbow." When you do that to kids, they grow up with an incredible sense of entitlement, and it's almost impossible for them to feel ashamed or guilty about anything.

I don't think you can erase what all human beings intuitively know: we should be perfect. We should love God and our neighbor. When I've been with people—no matter who they are or how they've been parented—when they are dying and they start to open up to me, it's like they are on a boat that goes out to sea at night. The person on the boat watches the lights dim slowly as the boat gets further away from shore. And when the last light goes out, there's almost a sense of regret: "I haven't lived the life I should have lived."

We all know deep down that we should be perfect. Someone may tell us, "Now that you believe in Jesus, all your sins are forgiven. There is no condemnation for you. God accepts you." But simply being told that a few times doesn't solve our problem. We go right back to works-righteousness (that's the natural, default mode of the human heart), and we subjectively stay in bondage to the law even though objectively we are no longer in bondage to it.

CHRISTIANS ARE IN BONDAGE TO THEIR SIN NATURE

"Sin shall no longer be your master, because you are not under the law, but under grace. What then? Shall we sin because we are not under the law but under grace? By no means!" (Rom. 6:14–15). It's very possible to not be under the law (i.e., one is objectively free from the law) but to be a slave to sin in practice. That is why Paul says, "Don't be a slave to sin!" Why? W. G. T. Shedd argues that sin is the suicidal action of the human will against itself.

> Sin contains an element of *servitude*,—that in the very act of transgressing the law of God there is a *reflex* action of the human will upon itself, whereby it becomes less able than before to keep that law. Sin is the suicidal action of the human will. It destroys the power to do right, which is man's true freedom.[2]

> Sin is the slow, and sure, and eternal suicide of a human will.[3]

In other words, when you commit a sin, you make it much easier to do it again and much harder to avoid and resist. Every time

---

[2] W. G. T. Shedd, *Sermons to the Natural Man* (New York: Scribner's, 1871), 202–3; cf. 229.
[3] W. G. T. Shedd, *Sermons to the Spiritual Man* (New York: Scribner's, 1884), 343.

you sin, you are destroying your ability to resist that sin. Every single time. "Sin is the suicidal action of the human will." Sin does not go away right away when you become a Christian. Even after you receive Christ and Christ accepts you and objectively removes your guilt, you are still tremendously in bondage to sin subjectively because that's how you have habitually lived.

CHRISTIANS ARE IN BONDAGE TO IDOLS[4]

If you love anything more than God, even though you believe in God, if there is anything in your life that is more important to your significance or security than God, then that is an idol—a kind of pseudo-god, a false god, a covenant master—and it will continually say, "Serve me or die," like Pharaoh. Objectively, Pharaoh was no longer the master of the Israelites. He said, "Go," and the Israelites left. But then Pharaoh said, "I want you back." This happens to all of us.

This can be true for your career, children, or ministry. If you want to be a good minister, that's fine. If things go wrong in your ministry, you'll be sad. If someone gets in the way of your doing a good job, you'll be mad. If there is a threat to the future of your ministry, you'll be afraid. That's normal.

But if your success in ministry is more important to your self-image than what God says about you, then it is functionally an idol. It's more important to you than God. You think, "I know that I'm an important person, that I'm valuable, because I'm a successful minister." Then when something goes wrong in your ministry, you're not just sad, but you melt down and completely lose it. When someone gets in the way of your ministry, you get not just angry but incredibly and vehemently angry. When there is a threat to the future of your ministry, you're not just afraid or worried but you're absolutely petrified and paralyzed with fear. Those emotions eat you up. Why? Those are your former covenant masters

---

[4] Cf. Timothy Keller, *Counterfeit Gods: The Empty Promises of Money, Sex, and Power, and the Only Hope That Matters* (New York: Dutton, 2009).

coming back, even though they are no longer your master. They come back to you and say, "Serve me or die. You need me. You can't live without me."

And that's the point. There is still slavishness in the Israelites' hearts. What you thought you were free from (and in one sense you *are* free from it) is still present to some degree. It comes back and rattles its sabers.

Years ago when I was trying to understand this, I read sermons by David Martyn Lloyd-Jones on Romans 6, and a particular illustration was illuminating.[5] Imagine, Lloyd-Jones said, that you were a slave in the southern United States before the Emancipation Proclamation. That means that you couldn't vote; you had no power; and somebody could beat you up and probably kill you. You didn't have rights. So if you were in town and some white person told you to do this or that and was abusive to you, you were very frightened and did anything he said.

Now it's ten years later, and the Emancipation Proclamation has been issued. You have rights. But you walk into town, and a white person starts to yell at you. Even though you know with your head, "Hey, I have some rights here," you're still scared and acting like a slave.

That actually is the condition of every Christian. You know, but you don't know. You know that you've been saved from slavery to sin and that you should be free. If you really believed in your heart what you know with your head (i.e., that there is no condemnation for you because you are in Christ Jesus, and God regards you as perfect because of Christ's righteousness), then you would not still be a slave in your heart to success or to what other people think of you. Technically and objectively, you're *not* a slave. But God has freed you from sins that you are *still* enslaved to.

We learn this in systematic theology class:

1. Justification (past): We are free from the penalty of sin.

---

[5] D. M. Lloyd-Jones, "Sermon Two," in *Romans: An Exposition of Chapter 6—The New Man* (Grand Rapids: Zondervan, 1972), 25–26.

2. Progressive sanctification (present): We are getting free from the power of sin.

3. Glorification (future): We will be free from the presence of sin.

You've heard that, but that is abstract. The exodus story models it. It's a picture of where we are. Redemption is about getting out of bondage, and it has layers. That is why the great songs talk about this. For example:

> Long my imprisoned spirit lay
> Fast bound in sin and nature's night;
> Thine eye diffused a quick'ning ray,
> I woke, the dungeon flamed with light;
> My chains fell off, my heart was free,
> I rose, went forth, and followed thee.[6]

That is true. We have those experiences, and yet every so often we find our hearts *not* free. Not free yet.

So salvation is about getting out. It's about getting out of bondage, and the bondage has layers. But what do we do about that?

SALVATION IS ABOUT HOW WE'RE GETTING OUT: CROSSING OVER BY GRACE

The Red Sea story is not just about what the Israelites get out of (bondage with layers) but also about how they get out (crossing over by grace). Here's how Moses replied to the fearful, complaining Israelites: "Moses answered the people, 'Do not be afraid. Stand firm and you will see the deliverance the LORD will bring you today. The Egyptians you see today you will never see again. The LORD will fight for you; you need only to be still'" (Ex. 14:13–14).

On the one hand, the principle of grace could not be clearer: "Stand still. God's going to do your fighting. Watch. You can't do it. You can't contribute to it. You can't do a thing. God's going to do the whole thing." When Moses says, "The LORD will fight for you;

---

6 Charles Wesley, "And Can It Be?," 1738.

you need only to be still" (14:14), he sounds like Paul: "to the one who does not work [cf. "be still"] but trusts God who justifies the ungodly, their faith is credited as righteousness" (Rom. 4:5). "Be still." Don't look at your works. Receive a complete salvation or deliverance, based not on your works but solely on Christ's works.

So that's the principle. But the exodus story also illustrates how that grace operates. It operates by crossing over. On one side of the Red Sea, the Israelites were within reach of their old false masters. They were under the sentence of death. Pharaoh said, "We're gonna get 'em or kill 'em." When the Israelites were on that side of the sea, they were reachable. They were still under the sentence of death. But when they tried to cross over—they succeeded in crossing over, yet when the Egyptians tried to cross over, an invisible warrior stopped them—the minute the Israelites crossed over, they crossed over from death to life. They crossed over from being under condemnation and the sentence of death to freedom.

This is one reason that our religion is absolutely and utterly different from every other religion. I've been saying this for over thirty years, and I regularly look at other religions to make sure that someone won't pull a "preacher gotcha" on me: "What about this religion over here?" and I'd have to say, "I haven't heard about that one. Let me read about it." No, every other religion is like building a bridge. You build a bridge by putting pylons down, and then you build the bridge over the pylons. And if you run out of money, it's the bridge to nowhere. There are a few like that. That is what every other religion is like. It's a process in which you are trying to get over to the other side. You never feel like you have arrived, but you're trying. In every other religion, people are trying to work their way across.

Not with Christianity. One minute you're not regenerate and the next minute you are. One minute you're not adopted and the next minute you are. Either you are regenerate and adopted, or you aren't. There's no process. Either you're in the kingdom of darkness, or God has brought you into the kingdom of the Son he loves (Col. 1:13). Think of all those statements and images that make Christianity unique: you either are a Christian or are not. "Very truly I tell you, whoever hears my word and believes him who sent me has eternal life and will not be judged but has *crossed over* from death to life" (John 5:24). Maybe John didn't actually have the exodus in mind, but Isaiah did:

> Was it not you who dried up the sea,
>   the waters of the great deep,
> who made a road in the depths of the sea
>   so that the redeemed might cross over? (Isa. 51:10)

This idea of crossing over—going from death to life immediately—is something that Martyn Lloyd-Jones used to use as a little test or analogy. When he was talking to individuals and trying to get a sense of where they were spiritually, he would ask them, "Are you a Christian?" If they said, "Well, I'm *trying*" (and many people said this, especially British people, who want to be modest), then Lloyd-Jones would proceed to explain that their answer indicated that they had no idea what Christianity is about at all. Not in the slightest. What makes one a Christian is a change in *status*.

1. You were in *that* kingdom, and now you're in *this* kingdom.
2. You were *out* of the family of God, and now you're *in* the family of God.
3. You were *not* born again, and now you're born again.
4. You were under God's wrath, and now you're justified.

Bang! It happens like that. Do you know the power of this? Here is Paul, who has killed people, and according to Romans 7, somehow at some point, God's law seems to have broken through his self-righteousness: "sin . . . through the commandment put me to death" (Rom. 7:11). We're not quite sure just what this autobiographical account means, but it seems like Paul began to realize what he had done.

Cate Blanchett acted in a 2002 movie called *Heaven*. It's not

a very well-known movie, but Cate Blanchett is one of the best ac-
tresses out there. It's a movie about a normal woman who is upset
about how a drug dealer is ruining the lives of children in a particular part of the city. The police won't listen to her, so she decides to
detonate a bomb in a drug dealer's office and kill him. But a night
watchman takes the bomb out, having discovered it in a waste bas-
ket, and puts it into an elevator where it explodes and kills four
people, including children. When Blanchett's character, a woman
who loves children and is doing this for the sake of children, learns
that she has killed children, she collapses. Because Blanchett is
such a great actress, you can see her collapse physically and emo-
tionally. She is a smoking wreck. In one sense she goes into a hell
of guilt and shame, and she never gets out of it.

Paul sensed that same guilt and shame, and yet he wrote,
"There is now no condemnation for those who are in Christ Jesus"
(Rom. 8:1). How could he say such a thing? Paul crossed over. He
didn't say, "Well, I've got a lot to atone for in my life." That is the
way the heart works for a person who is in bondage to the law. But
Paul was unbelievably humble about who he was, and it wasn't
false modesty. Why? Because he crossed over. He knew where he
stood. Of course, Paul had only begun to change on the inside, but
he knew where he stood with God. It's astonishing.

Somebody says, "Yeah, yeah, yeah. You're saved by grace apart
from works and your moral effort. But you've got to *believe*, don't
you? And you've *really* got to believe with *all* your heart because
salvation is by faith." Don't do that. Do you know what you're
doing? Even this text tells us something about that: "The waters were divided, and the Israelites went through the sea on dry
ground, with a wall of water on their right and on their left" (Ex.
14:21–22). The Israelites all crossed over, but that doesn't mean
that they all crossed over with the same disposition.

- Some walked through marveling at the walls of water: "Wow!
  Look at that! God is on our side! Eat your heart out, Egyptians! The Lord is fighting for us."

- Others were probably walking through like this: "I'm gonna die, I'm gonna die, I'm gonna die, *I'm gonna die!*"

Yet they all crossed over. Individual Israelites had different qualities of faith, but they were all equally saved. They were equally delivered. Why? Because you are not saved because of the quality of your faith. You are saved because of the *object* of your faith: the Redeemer, the God who is fighting for you. Everything about this text says, "Grace, grace, grace, grace. Crossing over is by grace."

Charles Spurgeon preached on Moses's saying, "Stand firm . . . . be still" and let God fight for you (Ex. 14:13–14). When you try to add to God's salvation, you subtract. If you try to merit God's salvation, you haven't believed in God at all; you are trusting yourself, even if you try to do only a little bit. At one point Spurgeon says:

> I dare say you will think it a very easy thing to *stand still*, but it is one of the postures which a Christian soldier learns not without years of teaching. I find that marching and quick marching are much easier to God's warriors than standing still. It is, perhaps, the first thing we learn in the drill of human armies, but it is one of the most difficult to learn under the Captain of our salvation. The apostle seems to hint at this difficulty when he says, "Stand fast, and having done all, still stand." To stand at ease in the midst of tribulation, shows a veteran spirit, long experience, and much grace.[7]

If you're a Christian, you've already crossed over. God has dealt with sin and death, and all of your other problems are merely flea bites in comparison. That's how you deal with your flea bites—by not looking at them as massive problems. Look at what God has already done for you.

So the Red Sea story illustrates that salvation is about getting out of bondage by crossing over by grace. But on what basis can we get out of bondage?

---

[7] "Direction in Dilemma," in Charles Spurgeon, *Metropolitan Tabernacle Pulpit*, vol. 9 (Pasadena, TX: Pilgrim Publications, 1969), 649ff.

SALVATION IS ABOUT WHY WE CAN GET OUT: THE MEDIATOR

Why is it possible for us to get out? The Egyptians went through the Red Sea and were devastated. But the Israelites crossed over. Why did the Israelites cross over safely?

Flood waters are significant. Most commentaries on Noah's flood say that God could have judged the world in many ways but that water is significant. Why? Go back to Genesis 1.

> In the beginning God created the heavens and the earth. Now the earth was formless and empty, darkness was over the surface of the deep, and the Spirit of God was hovering over the waters.
>
> And God said, "Let there be light," and there was light. God saw that the light was good, and he separated the light from the darkness. God called the light "day," and the darkness he called "night." And there was evening, and there was morning—the first day.
>
> And God said, "Let there be a vault between the waters to separate water from water." So God made the vault and separated the water under the vault from the water above it. And it was so. God called the vault "sky." And there was evening, and there was morning—the second day. (Gen. 1:1–8)

When the Spirit of God hovered over the waters, he brought order out of chaos. Water, not only in the Bible but also in many of the ancient cultures surrounding Israel at the time, represented chaos. Water was chaos and death. And yet God's creative Spirit came across the face of the waters, and he brought order out of chaos.

Therefore, when God used the flood to destroy the world in the time of Noah, what he was actually doing was making an appropriate judgment—what some people have called "de-creation." It was a reversal of creation. If you turn away from the Creator, you actually turn away from the goodness of creation. That unleashes disintegration and chaos.

If a husband hurts his wife, the wife may decide, "I am not going to forgive him." She might not say that, but she is so bitter and angry that she refuses to forgive. In a very small but very noticeable way, that unleashes chaos into their marriage until they obey God. The wages of sin is disintegration, which is another way of saying death.

What God was doing in the flood was unleashing the forces of chaos, which was a justifiable judgment. It was an appropriate judgment because when you turn away from the Creator you turn away from the goodness of creation and bring into your life de-creation and disintegration—the reversal of creation.

Many people have pointed out that that's what the plagues were. Just before the crossing of the Red Sea, God visited Egypt with plagues. But what were those plagues? The same thing. Pharaoh resisted the Creator, and Egypt experienced de-creation and disintegration such as darkness. The Red Sea could be called the eleventh plague because Egypt's sin unleashed the forces of chaos. God was judging Egypt. The flood waters represent what happens to you when you turn away from God.

We don't mind that because it happened to the Egyptians: "They got punished. Fine. The Egyptians were bad people, but the Israelites were good people." If you think that, you haven't read your Bible very carefully. You see Israel's childishness and petulance right here. They were not just fools; they were murderous fools. They simply did not have the same power as the Egyptians. They could not commit genocide right then because they did not have the power and technology. They were no better than the Egyptians.

The real question is why God's waters of judgment were standing up on both sides for the Israelites but crashing down on the Egyptians. Why didn't they come down on the Israelites?

Answer: the Israelites had a mediator. "Then the LORD said to

Moses, 'Why are you crying out to me?'" (Ex. 14:15). Commentators go two ways here.

1. Moses was crying out in rebellion like the Israelites earlier (Ex. 14:10–12), and God was rebuking Moses. This possibility is unlikely because the text does not indicate that Moses was rebelling. Some commentators argue, "Of course, Moses must have been rebelling, or God wouldn't have rebuked him," but *why?* Just before the Israelites crossed over, "Moses stretched out his hand over the sea, and all that night the LORD drove the sea back with a strong east wind and turned it into dry land" (Ex. 14:21).

2. Moses was one man who was so identified with the Israelites that their guilt was upon him, and he was so identified with God that God's power was coming through him. He was a man in the middle. He was so identified with the people that God rebuked him for their sin, and he was so identified with God that he was a vehicle for God's saving power.

But guess what? I know a better Mediator. And we don't have in Jesus Christ merely a mediator who is fully man and close to God. He is fully man and fully God. Not only that, we don't have a mediator whom God rebuked for any sin.

Here is what Jesus Christ understood. When Jonah was in the boat and the storm of God's wrath was about to sink the boat, Jonah turned to all the sailors and said, "This is a storm of God's wrath, and the only way you'll be saved is to throw me in. Throw me in, and you'll be saved." And the sailors threw Jonah in and were delivered. Jesus had the audacity to say, "Now something greater than Jonah is here" (Matt. 12:41). Jesus was talking about himself. Jesus Christ on the cross was thrown into the ocean of God's wrath. Jonah said, "I have been banished from your sight" (Jonah 2:4), which meant that he was hidden under the waves, and he felt forsaken by God. But when Jesus said, "My God, my God, why have you forsaken me?" (Matt. 27:46), he was being put under an ocean of God's wrath. All the plagues came down on Jesus. Darkness, for example, came down. Jesus was being de-created so that you and I could be re-created. Jesus received the reality that all these judgments such as flood waters point to.

That's why all the other things that we're talking about are possible. It's why we can be brought out. It's why we can keep going back to the well of Jesus's salvation to deal with layer after layer after layer of bondage. At one point Moses as the mediator went to God when God essentially said, "I've had it with these people." And Moses said, "Please forgive their sin—but if not, then blot me out of the book you have written" (Ex. 32:32). Yet God did not blot him out. But with our Mediator, Jesus, God did. Jesus is the ultimate Mediator, and it's why you and I can cross over.

CONCLUSION

Where are the children of Israel going? Sinai. One of the easiest ways to explain the gospel to somebody using the Old Testament is to say: "It wasn't that God gave them the law, and once they started to obey, he brought them out. He brought them out and then gave them the law. That's the gospel." It's not this: "Because I'm obeying God, now I'm saved." No, it's this: "Because I have been saved by God's free grace, now I want to obey God." Having been delivered, the Israelites were on their way to Sinai.

More than that, God said to Israel, "I am the LORD, who brought you up out of Egypt to be your God; therefore be holy, because I am holy" (Lev. 11:45). The more you meditate on what God has done and see the flood waters go over Jesus's head, the more holy you will be.

Sometimes people say to me, "Well, I know I shouldn't be doing this or that. But I know God forgives me." They don't know the first thing about forgiveness. Nobody who understands the grace of God would ever take sin lightly. The more you deal with the free grace of God and work it into your heart and understand that it has nothing to do with how you behave, the more radically that will change your behavior. God brought his people out of Egypt to take them to Sinai and give them the law so that they would be holy.

Why do you sin? Sometimes you sin simply because it's the easiest way. Let the gratitude you should have for God fill your hearts with so much joy that you say, "I'm not going to do that." But a large reason that we sin is our idols. We sin because we're being controlled by idols like fear. But the grace of God frees us from idols.

Some will then say, "It's all free and has nothing to do with my works or even the quality of my faith, so it doesn't matter how I live." If you think that, then you haven't even begun to come to grips with the grace of God. "Sin shall no longer be your master, because you are not under the law, but under grace. What then? Shall we sin because we are not under the law but under grace? By no means!" (Rom. 6:14–15).

When God says, "I brought you out of Egypt, so you should be holy," that's the same thing as, "We're saved by faith alone, but not by a faith that is alone." You're saved by faith apart from works, but if your works do not grow out of faith, then you don't have genuine faith.

That is found throughout the exodus story, too. It's amazing. It's the gospel.

Moses and Paul could have written the old hymn verse:

Well may the accuser roar
Of sins that I have done.
I know them all and thousands more,
Jehovah knoweth none.

Or Martin Luther's line: "What, have we nothing to do? No! Nothing!"[8] Be still, and realize that all your salvation is in Jesus. Be still. You have nothing to contribute at all. Look at him, and that will make you holy. And if you're not a Christian, it will make you a Christian.

Nathan Cole became a Christian listening to George Whitefield preach in Middletown, Connecticut, in 1744. He was practically

---

[8] Cited in *The Journal of the Reverend John Wesley* (London: Epworth, 1938), 1:476.

illiterate, but he wrote about what it was like to hear Whitefield preach and how he became a Christian: "My hearing him preach gave me a heart wound. By God's blessing my old foundation was broken up, and I saw that my righteousness would not save me."[9]

If that's beginning to happen to you now, go on and don't stop until you know what this means: "The blood of Jesus, his Son, purifies us from all sin" (1 John 1:7).

---

[9] Quoted in George Leon Walker, *Some Aspects of the Religious Life of New England with Special Reference to Congregationalists* (New York: Silver, Burdett and Co., 1897), 91.

3

FROM A FOREIGNER TO KING JESUS

Ruth

Alistair Begg

I recently came across a book review that described the author's work as "the supreme example of purposeful boredom in literary form." In stark contrast, the book of Ruth is arguably one of the loveliest short stories ever written. It is literary art and theological insight at its very finest.

Just as jewelers routinely present diamonds on a dark velvet cloth as a means of showing the gems at their sparkling best, so here against the dark and somber background of the period of the judges, the book of Ruth shines. The time of the judges was at the very least unstable. If there had been blogs in those days, they would have been filled with reports of civil unrest, moral decay, religious declension, and unchecked corruption. This is the recurring cycle throughout the book of Judges, which ends with the observation, "In those days Israel had no king; everyone did as he saw fit" (Judg. 21:25).[1]

Then with the turn of a page we discover another side to the story here in the book of Ruth. We learn how God was at work in a very unusual way in a sequence of events involving a Bethlehem

---

[1] Unless otherwise indicated, Scripture quotations in this chapter are from the 1984 edition of *The Holy Bible, New International Version*®, NIV®. Copyright © 1973, 1978, 1984 by Biblica, Inc.™ Used by permission. All rights reserved worldwide.

farmer, a foreigner from Moab, and a lady who had faced a triple bereavement.

If these four short chapters were made into a movie, and if we were responsible for the musical score, it would surely begin in a minor key with the tone of a lament. A plaintive background refrain would epitomize the sadness and disappointment that unfolds in just a few verses. The camera would linger on the face of Naomi, a lonely lady living in a foreign land in her declining years with no children to care for her and no grandchildren to cheer her spirits. Who, then, could ever dream that Naomi's sad predicament would, in the providence of God, lead first to the conversion of her daughter-in-law Ruth and through that lineage to the birth of David, the great king of Israel, and then to the Messiah himself? Although this is not the main emphasis of the book of Ruth, the story provides an opportunity to make clear to the Naomis of our culture and in our churches that God defends widows and cares about their suffering (Deut. 10:18; Ps. 68:6).

PREACHING CHRIST FROM THE OLD TESTAMENT

CHALLENGES

How should we preach Christ and the gospel from the book of Ruth? Learning to do this is the journey of a lifetime. "No man knows how to preach. . . . It is right that the vast difficulty of the task should humble you. It is wrong that it should paralyze you."[2]

Our listeners should be able to follow the progression of thought that introduces them to the person and work of Jesus, in Old Testament narrative. That is not as straightforward as it sounds, and it involves hard work on our part to ensure that we do not lead them on a theological wild-goose chase! As a young minister I made a number of false starts in attempting to teach Ruth because I was not yet clear in my own mind about the way in which the various lines came together in Jesus. If there is fog in

---

[2] James S. Stuart, *The Heralds of God*, Warrack Lectures on Preaching (New York: Scribner's, 1946), 104–5.

the pulpit, we should not expect clarity in the pew. When it comes to our preaching Christ in all the Scriptures, our congregation should not be mystified by our wizardry, exclaiming, "How did he do that!" Rather they should be edified by our clarity, declaring, "That makes sense to me." We should have confidence in unfolding the Scriptures in this way because Jesus explained to his followers that the Law of Moses and the Prophets and the Psalms (the threefold division of the Hebrew Bible) point to him (Luke 24:44).

ASSUMPTIONS

We come to Old Testament narrative with certain assumptions. (At least, I assume we do!)

1. We assume that God has acted in human history both to reveal and to redeem.
2. We assume that God has raised up prophets and apostles to provide in Holy Scripture both the record and the interpretation of God's intervention.
3. We assume that the preacher's message, both in its content and in its aim, is to set forth the Scriptures. And in setting forth the Scriptures that speak of Christ, preachers set forth Christ.
4. We assume that the need for the proper Christian use of the Old Testament is urgent. Some of us have been scared away from the Old Testament by scientific and historical criticism, and others are hindered by certain models of dispensationalism.
5. We assume that we will be helped if we learn (as Alec Motyer suggests) to read the Bible from back to front. It is easier to find the tributaries if we stand at the mouth of the river and then work back from there. The Bible is like a detective novel where all these various themes are woven together for a lengthy period of time until finally there is a great denouement that makes sense of all the interwoven pieces. The Bible is like a two-act drama where if you show up for Act 1 but leave before Act 2, you will be left wondering how it concludes; and if you come for Act 2 but miss Act 1, you will

annoy everyone around you by constantly saying, "Who are these people, and why are they here?" B. B. Warfield used the analogy of the Old Testament as being like a richly furnished but dimly lit room; the contents become clear only when the light is turned on in the person and work of Jesus.[3] So, for example, we need the book of Hebrews in order to understand Leviticus. We can't make sense of the prophets today without the New Testament. And we can't understand the message of Ruth apart from the coming of Jesus.

OBSERVATIONS

Let me add two observations: First, the Old Testament Scriptures can and should mean more to us than they did to the people of the Old Testament because we live in the light of their Christian fulfillment. Once again our pattern in this is clearly Christ addressing Cleopas in Luke 24. It is hard to imagine Jesus doing what he did in that passage and leaving out the book of Ruth.

Second, the genre of the text should determine how we proclaim Christ. Our exposition will go badly wrong if we can preach exactly the same kind of sermon regardless of the genre—Old Testament narrative or New Testament epistle or Gospel. The genre determines how the whole story unfolds. So when we approach the book of Ruth, we must immerse ourselves in the sights and sounds and smells and tastes. The book of Ruth is in that sense "sensual" (not in the sense of arousing erotic notions). It is full of the senses. The book is crafted so wonderfully that it introduces little glimpses here and there that give the reader the sense that there is something more that is beyond this if we will simply read on. Ruth invites us to feel deeply, and our understanding of the gospel will enable us to apply the text properly.

Tiny stories are hugely appealing in our time. Adults have a peculiar sense of nostalgia for the phrases that the *Oxford English Dictionary* says have introduced and concluded stories since the

---

[3] See Benjamin B. Warfield, "The Biblical Doctrine of the Trinity," in *Biblical Doctrines*, The Works of Benjamin B. Warfield 2 (New York: Oxford University Press, 1932), 141–42.

fourteenth century: "Once upon a time"; "And they all lived happily ever after."

Did you find it interesting that Dreyfus and Kelly, the philosophy professors from Berkeley and Harvard, sought to bring their philosophy down to this level by writing a book called *All Things Shining*?[4] In it they suggest that it is in the little glimpses and moments of time that we may be able to find significance. In reading the classic novels we may find meaning and purpose. If we have been feeling gloomy, we may find an antidote in reading *Moby Dick*, for example.

Here is a way for us to say to people, "You don't need to read the Western classics to find meaning in a secular age. I've got a classic for you right here: the book of Ruth." I've done this from time to time when I've met people named Ruth, perhaps in a restaurant or on a plane: "Ruth, do you know there's a book called Ruth?"

"No!"

"Oh, yes. It's a great book. You should read it. It's short, but it's super."

THREE CHARCOAL SKETCHES

I'm going to present three charcoal sketches from the book of Ruth.

My art teacher in grammar school was Mr. Walker. When I would ask him for help with an assignment he would take his pencil and begin to sketch, and as he did so he would say: "I'll get you started, Begg, but I'm not going to do it for you." I am taking a leaf out of his book and will leave you to fill out the picture on your own.

CHARCOAL SKETCH 1:
THREE WOMEN ON THE ROAD TO SOMEWHERE

> With her two daughters-in-law she left the place where she had been living and set out on the road that would take them back to the land of Judah. (Ruth 1:7)

---

[4] Hubert Dreyfus and Sean Kelly, *All Things Shining: Reading the Western Classics to Find Meaning in a Secular Age* (New York: Free Press, 2011).

This scene on the roadway is not so much a Kodak moment as it is a Kleenex moment. The dialogue is full of pathos, and we should not think of the tears in terms of polite sniffles but rather of great breath-catching, heart-rending sobs.

The backdrop to the scene on the road is that of poor choices, sad experiences, and deep disappointments that are intertwined in these women's lives. In the book of Judges God warned his people that if they were unfaithful to his covenant promises, the consequences would be dire. Disregarding the warning the people rebelled and found themselves facing famine. Yet, because of his loving-kindness, his *hesed* love, God held out to his people the promise of forgiveness and grace if they would return to him in repentance and faith.

This huge drama is played out here in a microcosm as the camera zooms in on the family of Elimelech. Elimelech's name means "the Lord is king." Ironically, he did not feel the Lord to be king over the circumstances of the famine. Had he done so, he would have stayed put in Bethlehem. But instead he left Bethlehem (which, ironically, means "house of bread") and set off for Moab. Instead of trusting the Lord with all his heart, he relied on his own insight. Pragmatism won out over obedient faith.

It was Naomi who provided the theological explanation for these events: "The Lord's hand has gone out against me" (Ruth 1:13). In other words, "I can't explain my life apart from God's intervening work." They had made certain decisions, and in light of these found themselves in this place and condition.

But God had kindly provided food for his people in Bethlehem (Ruth 1:6). Consequently, Naomi decided to return home. Naomi's journey is aptly summarized in this stanza from George Herbert:

> Or if I stray, he doth convert
> And bring my mind in frame:
> And all this not for my desert,
> But for his holy name.[5]

---

[5] George Herbert, "The 23d Psalm," accessed at http://www.georgeherbert.org.uk/Archive/selected _work_09.html.

Consider the scene as she stood in between Moab and Bethlehem, encouraging her two daughters-in-law to return to their homeland where they would find security. She urged them to count the cost. They had to choose: "Yahweh plus nothing in Bethlehem or everything minus Yahweh in Moab."[6] With that choice set before them, Orpah returned home, but Ruth refused to follow Orpah even though Naomi pressed her, "Look, you've still got a chance to return with your sister-in-law, Orpah. You could catch up with her now. Go back with her."

She couldn't be persuaded to return. This was essentially Ruth's conversion. How do we actually fathom this? How do we plumb the depths of divine persuasion? How do we understand this mystery? Presented with the exact same circumstance and urgings from the same lips of the same lady, one went back to Moab and the other used the language of the covenant and said, in effect, "No, I can't go back because I'm no longer what I once was. I am no longer trusting in the gods to which my sister-in-law has now returned. Don't ask me to leave you. I'm going where you go, and from now on your God is my God."

God calls people to respond to his unerring loving-kindness and grace, and people must trust God as Ruth did. God does not believe for us. We believe. And Ruth believed. Do you? Are you a believer? Have you turned your back on the substitute gods of the world by which you live by nature? Have you been embraced by the loving-kindness of God as it has been shown to you in so many different ways?

Some years ago when Jim Boice was still alive, the Alliance of Confessing Evangelicals visited Harvard University in Cambridge, Massachusetts. I was scheduled to speak on a Saturday morning, and early that morning I was studying my Bible in a deserted coffee shop. A Chinese student at Harvard came into the shop, and when she saw my Bible, she asked, "Are you a Christian?"

I replied, "Yes, I am."

---

[6] Sinclair Ferguson, *Faithful God: An Exposition of the Book of Ruth* (Bridgend, Wales: Bryntirion, 2005), 38.

She said, "I'm a Christian, too."

When I asked how she had come to trust in Christ, she answered memorably, "I entered through narrow gate."

That is what happened in our text. Ruth entered through the narrow gate.

God was reaching into Ruth's life across the barriers of race, and her picture was painted in the great scene in Revelation: persons "from every tribe and language and people and nation" (Rev. 5:9). Those people are worshiping King Jesus, who descended from this woman Ruth.

CHARCOAL SKETCH 2:
THE NAME OF THE MAN IS BOAZ

The name of the man I worked with today is Boaz. (Ruth 2:19)

I grew up in Glasgow, which in the 1960s had a Jewish population second only to London's in the United Kingdom. Many of my friends were Jewish, and I was often in their homes and learned to appreciate the caring role of their mothers. When I read of Naomi, I see them in my mind's eye: "Where did you glean today? And where have you worked?" (Ruth 2:19, ESV). Learning that Ruth worked with Boaz, Naomi praised God, whose kindness had forsaken neither the living nor the dead. We might imagine her saying: "Oh, Boaz! Boaz is a nice boy, Naomi. Boaz is a kinsman redeemer. You should stay in his field, Naomi. That is a good field."

It is at this point in our "film version" of the story that the music under the dialogue would change from a minor to a major key. Famine has been replaced with a rich harvest. The plaintive sounds of the lone bag piper have given way to the arrival of the minstrels! The music changes because the mood has changed. The story is not complete, but in the barley harvest we are given a sneak preview of the fullness and richness that is in the offing. To this point neither Naomi nor Ruth could conceive of all that God had in store for them.

Chapter 2 begins by introducing this new character: "Now

Naomi had a relative on her husband's side, from the clan of Elimelech, a man of standing, whose name was Boaz" (v. 1), causing the reader to ask, "I wonder what he's like and if he has a big part in this story."

Do you ever wish that you didn't know how stories like this end so that you could read them with an initial sense of discovery? (Think too of the story of Joseph.) Maybe if I live long enough, I will have forgotten the endings of most of them.

Ruth had been learning how the God of Abraham, Isaac, and Jacob made provision for the poor. So Ruth's request was based upon the fact of God's providence: "Let me go to the fields and pick up the leftover grain behind anyone in whose eyes I find favor" (2:2). The word "favor" sends the reader in a particular direction.

> Why have I found such *favor* in your eyes that you notice me—a foreigner? (2:10).

> "May I continue to find favor in your eyes, my lord," she said. "You have given me comfort and have spoken kindly to your servant—though I do not have the standing of one of your servant girls." (2:13)

This loving-kindness of God runs all the way through this narrative. God is providentially at work in all free human choices including the very field in which Ruth "happened to come to."

The drama intensifies at the end of chapter 2 and the beginning of chapter 3. Naomi suggests that Ruth pursue Boaz, who is a kinsman redeemer.

How do we communicate the concept of a kinsman redeemer to people today? We mustn't say more than we need to, but we mustn't say less than is required. The challenge is to get it clear in our own minds so that we can briefly explain that the word translated "relative" ("kinsman," NASB) refers to a redeemer and is used of Yahweh himself in other contexts. Yahweh is the divine "next of kin" for his people. He comes alongside them as the one who both has revealed himself and will redeem his people.

So Boaz has the right to intervene in the circumstances of Naomi and Ruth. He can meet their needs and treat them as if they were his very own.

Ruth would understand this. The marriage of Boaz and Ruth gets to the very heart of this concept. That is why when Paul speaks of marriage, he speaks of the great mystery between Christ and his church, an amazing marriage in which God has taken the initiative. This illustrates the glory of the gospel because it foreshadows Christ, who in himself is the only one who has the right to take and bear as his own all that spoils and ruins, all the loss, hurt, disaster, alienation, brokenness, and sinful messed-up-ness of things. This physician heals by taking to himself our diseases. He bears them in himself.

CHARCOAL SKETCH 3:
A SON HAS BEEN BORN

> Then Naomi took the child, laid him in her lap and cared for him. (Ruth 4:16)

The women of Bethlehem gave quite a baby shower at the birth of this son! They had witnessed the sorry arrival of Naomi and Ruth recorded in chapter 1, and now they led the praise as they saw the hand of God in this provision. In the everyday events of village life and among ordinary people, God was at work. Naomi had announced, "The Lord has brought me back empty" (1:21), but here we see her with her hands full as a result of God's provision. Ruth had turned her back on all that represented security in her homeland only to discover true security in the God of Israel, "under whose wings," said Boaz, "you have come to take refuge" (2:12). The Lord who had visited his people and given them food 1:6) had given Ruth a son.

But this story does not end with Ruth and Boaz sending out their birth announcements or even with the pictures of a happy grandmother cradling the boy who had the potential to put some zip into her closing years. Instead it finishes with a family tree, the genealogy of David the king of Israel. The women prayed for this child in Naomi's lap, "May his name be renowned in Israel!" (4:14, ESV). Little did they know of the extent to which their prayer was to be answered.

One of my friends recently reminded me that the providences of God are seldom, if ever, self-interpreting. In other words, the explanation for what happens in our lives is usually quite literally "beyond us." We see that here in the lives of these central characters. Was it right for Elimelech to forsake the "house of bread" in search of bread? Had he not done so, his sons would not have married the Moabite girls. If that had not happened, Ruth would not have come to Bethlehem, and there would have been no marriage to Boaz, and thus no Obed, and so no Jesse, and thus no David. But it doesn't even end there. We find this family tree in the first chapter of Matthew and we read on to the staggering conclusion: ". . . the father of Joseph, the husband of Mary, of whom was born Jesus, who is called Christ" (Matt. 1:16).

We began by noticing that this story is set at a time when there was no king in Israel. It was in that context and in the lives of ordinary people that God was preparing the way for Jesus, the King of kings and the Lord of lords. In the experience of famine and darkness he was paving the way for Jesus, the bread of life and the light of the world!

CONCLUSION

In *All Things Shining*, Dreyfus and Kelly observe that when you search for shining moments, you must be aware that they do not cohere or combine to make any sense at all. That's existentialism.

But Ruth is a different kind of story. In Jesus all things hold together. He, as the Mediator of a new covenant, extends his blessing to sinners by bringing them into a covenantal relationship with himself. And if they will turn to him, he will welcome them with open arms.

John Calvin writes that when we have preached in this way,

then we show that the only haven of safety [cf. Ruth 2:12: "under whose wings you have come to take refuge"] is in the mercy of God, as manifested in Christ, in whom every part of our salvation is complete. As all mankind are, in the sight of God, lost sinners, we hold that Christ is their only righteousness, since, by His obedience, He has wiped off our transgressions; by His sacrifice, appeased the divine anger; by His blood, washed away our sins [stains]; by His cross, borne our curse; and by His death, made satisfaction for us. We maintain that in this way man is reconciled in Christ to God the Father, by no merit of his own, by no value of works, but by gratuitous mercy.[7]

---

[7] John Calvin, *Reply to Cardinal Sadoleto.*

4

WHEN YOU DON'T KNOW WHAT TO DO

Psalm 25

James MacDonald

When I was assigned Psalm 25 to preach on, I couldn't decide honestly whether it was a gift or a gauntlet. I didn't know if the challenge was "Let's see you preach Christ from *this* kind of passage!" So I approached the opportunity with a trepidation factor. But as I've studied Psalm 25, I now really do think this assignment was a gift. And I'm grateful.

Since I've been asked to offer this message as part of a wider theme of "Preaching Christ from the Old Testament," I want to make sure that we're not assuming too much in our departure point. Before we can preach Christ from the Old Testament, we have to just preach. Second Timothy 4 is very instructive about our responsibility to preach the Word. Paul makes it clear to young Timothy that his personal life and his public pursuits must be saturated with the Scriptures. It's probably worth noting that all who preached Christ *in* the New Testament pretty much preached him *from* the Old Testament. So when Paul tells Timothy, "Until I come, devote yourself to the public reading of Scripture, to exhortation, to teaching" (1 Tim. 4:13),[1] he is directing his envoy to deliver the content of the Old Testament to people, particularly as it applies to Christ.

---

[1] Unless otherwise indicated, Scripture quotations in this chapter are from the English Standard Version.

The Second Helvetic Confession from the sixteenth century declares, *praedicatio verbi dei est verbum dei*, which means, "The preaching of the Word of God is the Word of God." Calvin said, "God . . . deigns to consecrate . . . the tongues of men in order that his voice may resound in them."[2] Many pulpits today are not preaching the Word of God. They're between red-faced sermonic rants and self-indulgent intellectual meanderings through the dark forest of "it seems to me." Many are not actually heralding the Word that God has given. What our nation is hungry for, what our world is crying out for is "thus says the Lord." We have to come back to faithfully proclaiming God's Word.

So, yes, preach the Word. And then preach Christ from the Word. Preach Christ from all sixty-six books, from Genesis 1:1 to Revelation 22:21. Let's preach Christ from the Word of God.

My mom went to heaven last summer. She died of ALS, and she suffered greatly. Going through that experience has caused me to treasure in a deeper way what it meant for my mother to get forty little elementary school kids down in the basement every Tuesday afternoon after school and teach the Word of God to us. And I treasure more than I ever could have as a child the chorus that she taught us: "The Bible is the written Word of God," we used to sing.

> The Bible is the written Word of God.
> It tells about the living Word of God.
> On every page, on every line you'll find the Son of God divine.
> If you want to learn to know the King of kings,
> If you want to learn of all the heavenly things,
> Read the Book; learn the Book, let the Book teach you.[3]

That was a great chorus. I love what it's saying. And so I love the theme before us: preaching Christ from the Old Testament.

---

[2] John Calvin, *Institutes of the Christian Religion*, ed. John T. McNeill, trans. Ford Lewis Battles (Philadelphia: Westminster, 1960), 4.1.5.
[3] A chorus written by Ruth H. Munce (daughter of Grace Livingstone Hill) and widely used in Bible clubs under the permission of Percy and Don Crawford.

BACKGROUND

Open your Bibles to Psalm 25. We understand that you don't just rip open the Bible and start reading it. You've got to understand what you have in your hands, and so I shall mention four things by way of background in regard to Psalm 25.

IT'S A PSALM

First, at the risk of stating the obvious but to acknowledge what we are about to explore, it's a psalm. The Psalms are the most quoted Old Testament book in the New Testament. Isaiah is a distant second. The New Testament quotes Isaiah about 50 times and the Psalms over 400 times.

One of our authors on the Gospel Coalition website said recently that the Psalms are the songbook of Jesus. What a guiding perspective to have as we gaze into this great book. Psalm 25 is a song written over three thousand years ago. Of the 150 psalms, 100 name the author; of those, 75 are attributed to David. This is one of those Davidic psalms.

IT'S A POEM

Second, this psalm is a poem. The Psalms are ancient Hebrew poetry, not rhyming like we would think of poetry, but artistic structures. There are two main poetic features in Psalm 25. One visual artistic flair is that it's an acrostic. Almost every verse begins with the successive letter of the Hebrew alphabet.

The other poetic feature is that the truths come in couplets, repeating the same message with different words. We learned in seminary this is called *synonymous parallelism*. Each truth is stated twice, the second time in a slightly altered way for emphasis and beauty. That's what's happening again and again as we go through this poetic song of David.

There's a pattern in Psalm 25 that combines the typical language of prayer and creed. Back and forth: addressing God directly (vv. 1–7, 11, 16–22), then addressing a human audience (vv. 8–10,

12–15); prayer, creed, prayer. David is keenly aware of God's attentiveness to his words but also acknowledges that others will hear and use his song.

IT'S ABOUT DESPAIR

Third, the subject of the psalm is crying out in desperation and despair. It's David in pursuit of total trust upon God. And so the title I've given to this message is "When You Don't Know What to Do."

Have you ever had a time in your life when you didn't know what to do? What do you do when you don't know what to do? The answer to that question is to trust. David had to learn and practice the truth that when you don't know what to do, you trust. And if it was a good enough lesson for David, you know it's a good enough lesson for you and me. Sometimes we don't know what to do, and we should trust! That's what's coming to us now in Psalm 25.

I have found it helpful to distinguish two main emphases in this psalm. On the one hand, there are "learning" themes—things we need to learn about God so we trust him better. But on the other hand, there are "leaning" themes in the psalm as well—ways of trusting God or things that we do that amount to trusting God. Some of what this psalm says teaches us what to *learn*; some of it teaches us how to *lean*. But all of it is about this matter of trusting God better, especially when you don't know what to do.

IT'S A PLEA FROM A BROKENHEARTED MAN

Past the genre of the psalm, past the literary device of the poetry, past the pattern and structure, this learning exercise remains in essence the plea of a brokenhearted man. As you study God's Word, don't ever let your analysis cause paralysis. This psalm is a person's life. This is a person's relationship with God that is modeling under the inspiration of the Spirit something very important for us. And though we don't know for certain the exact biographical setting of Psalm 25, this is a plea. This is a cry from a heartbroken man, a king.

While some debate the background for Psalm 25, the internal clues narrow the possible times in David's life that could have produced this intense expression. The text certainly supports that David is in a very desperate place. He speaks of his enemies and his foes. He speaks of treachery as well as hate. He speaks of the threat of ambush and profound loneliness and sorrow. David has been betrayed. He's crushed in his spirit. He's devastated by what has happened to him.

In my twenties I probably thought that I had been crushed. I never had been. I'm sure I thought in my thirties that I had been crushed. But I was still fairly clueless. It wasn't until my late forties that I began to understand what it is to be crushed, and I came to realize that a psalm like this can come only from a person who knows what it is to be crushed in a vise.

Some suggest that this psalm presupposes David's experience with Saul, but in the text he says, "Remember not the sins of my youth" (v. 7). So he is not a young man when he is going through this, and that autobiographical note has generally led scholars to agree that the backdrop for this psalm is Absalom's betrayal.

That story begins in 2 Samuel 3. Absalom was David's third son by his second wife. David's already in trouble in the marriage category. This is not God's best plan. We have that in Genesis: one man and one woman for a lifetime. David is already off plan. And born to this second wife is this third son, Absalom.

Eventually David's kids grow up, and by 2 Samuel 13, his first son, Amnon, rapes one of his daughters, Tamar. His third son, Absalom, is angry at his half-brother Amnon for what he did to his sister Tamar. But his rage is also directed at the father, who is so incredibly passive that he doesn't deal with the sin of his firstborn son. So Absalom hates his brother and murders him. Then David banishes Absalom rather than confronting him. He doesn't deal with the tragic escalating results of his own passivity. He just puts Absalom away from himself.

After a long period of time, Absalom begs his way back into Jerusalem and then maneuvers his way back into the palace. And finally at the end of chapter 14, the king kisses the murderous son but puts him out again. The seething conflict has not been settled—just placed out of sight.

By 2 Samuel 15:1, Absalom says, in effect, "Not me. Not this. No more." So he gets in his chariot and starts rallying the people around, carrying out a calculated PR campaign. As the people come to David for counsel to solve problems, Absalom steps in and says, "Yeah, I know a little bit about that. Listen, the king's kind of old and busy. You might want to talk to me about your situation." So more and more, the hearts of the men go after Absalom (chaps. 15–16). The people follow him and look to him as the de facto king. It's a bloodless coup, a mutiny. Absalom pulls off a betrayal of the highest order.

We can picture David writing Psalm 25 on the run. He has fled from the palace and taken with him the few friends and soldiers who have not betrayed him. The king of Israel is encamped outside the royal city, hiding in his old wilderness haunts. People have to bring him food so that he can survive while he tries to avoid a conflict that would kill his son.

If you're imagining all this, the description is like a Jerry Springer episode. If you are watching, you say, "Why doesn't David kill the kid? The boy's a lost cause." You say that—until it is your dearest friend or your closest ministry partner or your spouse or one of *your* kids. For if you are *living* it, those days are crushing, devastating, and despair-inducing.

Joab, the king's general, just cannot understand why David responds as he does to the news of Absalom's death. David weeps and says, "O my son, Absalom, my son, my son Absalom! Would I had died instead of you" (2 Sam. 18:33). The reason Joab cannot comprehend this is because he hasn't been crushed as David has been. This is the most plausible circumstance that leads to the writing of Psalm 25.

EXPOSITION

Let's go through this wonderful passage.

VERSES 1-3

Verse 1

The opening verse states the theme of the entire psalm:

> To you, O LORD, I lift up my soul.
> O my God, in you I trust. (v. 1)

"Soul" commonly means "the seat of desire," the internal, nonmaterial part of man, but it can mean the whole being. David comes in desperation, and he lifts up all that he is to God.

Verse 2

David then launches into the content of his prayer: "Let me not be put to shame" (v. 2). How clear is that prayer? "Put to shame" means "to fall into disgrace," "to be shamed." *Don't let this end badly, God.* David is crying out in desperation. He's afraid of being shamed. He saw how Saul died. He's afraid that his enemies are going to gloat over him.

Have you ever been afraid—really scared that something was going to happen to you? I've been a Chicago Blackhawks fan all my life. In 2010, some friends and I went to their game in Philadelphia to see the Stanley Cup final. And you've heard about Philadelphia fans; they're not like fans anywhere else. I was embarrassed and frightened, so although I put on my Chicago Blackhawks jersey, over it I wore a Philadelphia Flyers jersey. So when I was walking to the game, all my brothers were getting called out, but I sailed through.

But when I got inside the arena, I felt kind of bold. So when I ran into Mark Giangreco, the Channel 2 newscaster from Chicago, I did something that wasn't very smart. I pulled off the Flyers jersey on camera! I revealed my true Blackhawk-fan self. That seemed like a great idea, but all the Flyers fans watched my sudden transformation. So now I'm looking around, and I would have been better off just to wear the Blackhawk jersey in. Now I was Enemy Number 1. I *heard* it! And I'm telling you, when the Hawks won, Blackhawk fans were getting punched and shoved; it was crazy. I said to myself, "This is not going to end well." And all the guys I walked in with, they were hard to find at that point.

Take that and multiply the fear by a factor that's unimaginable, and you will begin to glimpse what David is feeling when he says, "Let me not be put to shame." *God, don't let this go where it looks like it's going.*

Verse 3

David is learning: "Wait a minute. What am I so stressed out about?" Verse 3:

> Indeed, none who wait for you shall be put to shame;
>   they shall be ashamed who are wantonly treacherous.

It might not look good today. Your son may be pretty far out there. Your test results may look very bad. Your heart may be in a vise over some crushing reality. It may feel like shame is inevitable, but nothing is over yet. None who wait for the Lord will be put to shame; they won't fall into disgrace. Not ultimately. Not in the end. Not when the Lord is done.

And so our first main thought here is part of the lesson we've got to learn in this passage: *I don't know where this is going. I don't know how it ends exactly, but here I understand that in the end—"no shame."* Not when it's over. Not when God is done.

But some are going to "be ashamed." As I seek to trust God more and better, something that I desperately need to learn is wrapped up in that word "wantonly." The NASB and NIV say "without cause." But is there ever an excuse or a reason to be betrayed? No one deserves what David is experiencing. Pastors don't deserve betrayal. Parents don't deserve betrayal, and neither do children. How comforting to embrace and learn to trust the God who never betrays his people. There is no shame in suffering the shameful betrayals of others.

VERSES 4-5

Verse 4

Notice God's way in verse 4:

> Make me to know your ways, O LORD;
>   teach me your paths.
> Lead me in your truth and teach me.

The beginning of verse 5 really could go with 4. There, I think, is the parallelism. Notice the plurals: "your *ways* . . . your *paths*." This is not a prayer for specific guidance. This is a petition to understand God's pattern. "Make me to learn your ways, God." God has his ways.

Hosea 14:9 calls us to wisdom and understanding, "for the ways of the LORD are right." Isaiah 55 tells us that the ways of the Lord are as high as the heavens are above the earth—high above our ways. God has different ways of doing things. He has some very different paths for us to travel.

In effect, David is saying:

- "I can't get through this if you don't help me understand your ways better."
- "Really, God? You're in this? This is your way? Really? This is the way you want this?"
- "I want to understand God's way, but I'm not seeing it right now."

April 2008 and April 2009 were the two worst months of my life. In God's providence they were also the months of the Gospel Coalition meetings, and in those two years I was in the throes of finding out that I had prostate cancer. Our church was in major turmoil and upheaval at the leadership level, but I couldn't talk about it. At home we were going through the best and worst of growing pains as our children faced all the challenges of adulthood. David's words, "I am lonely and afflicted" (Ps. 25:16b) put what I was feeling into words.

I forced myself to go and sit in on some of the sessions, and at one of the breaks, a friend who has been a real pastor to me and a pastor in our area noticed me over in a corner. It was dark. He came over to me, and he put his hand on my shoulders, like he would. (Pastors need pastors too.) He said, "How are you, brother?" in his beautiful English accent. I just hung my head and started to sob. I said, "I don't know what to do. I don't know what to do."

If you've never been at the place where the trials are so significant that you don't even know what to do, then you don't understand Psalm 25. David is pleading, "God, I'm not seeing it. I know you have ways, but I have to learn them because everything that's happening makes no sense to me at all." A big part of trusting is learning this truth: trust must extend past understanding. "I just don't get it Lord, but I'm trusting you."

Verse 5

In August 2009, I taught Psalm 25 in my church. Ninety-eight percent of our people knew nothing about what I was facing and dealing with, but my circumstances sure caused me to understand verse 5, where David asks,

> Lead me in your truth and teach me,
>   for you are the God of my salvation.

"Salvation" can have many meanings in Scripture. Here David is saying, You're the God who gets me out. I wait for you. No one but you can get me out of this. You are the God of my salvation!

When you say that you are waiting, that means that you are accepting God's wise timing. You are confessing, "I'm not fussing. I'm not fuming. I'm not fixing." You're not thinking in the back of your mind, "Oh, I could do a few things to get me out of this situation. I've got some insights. I might say some things. I could make some moves. I could get some balls rolling. I could take hold of this if I had to."

I say this to my own shame. I've had to learn the meaning of the words: "The anger of man does not produce the righteousness of God" (James 1:20). We learn as pastors and we learn as parents that when you want righteousness for somebody more than you want to be righteous, that's not going anywhere good. That lesson is what you are displaying when you say, "I'm waiting on God for my salvation. This is about his ways and his paths. He has to get me out of this narrow place."

Three years ago today my world was just about as dark as it could possibly be. But today, praise God for his faithfulness, our church is flourishing. My health has returned. I have discovered the unspeakable joy of grandchildren and the fatherly pride in seeing my children following the Lord. And I can't stop praising God.

But it was not like that *then*. I remember two years ago I was going out for dinner with some people I hadn't met before. Another good pastor-friend in the city—it's kind of cool how we pastor each other—was driving me over to the place where we were going to eat dinner, and I couldn't even get out of the car. He asked, "What's wrong?" And I sat there in the car and just poured out my heart to him. I told him everything. He listened quietly and intently. And then he prayed for me. Have you ever had someone really pray for you? I pray that you have someone pray for you like that! He sat there with his hands on the steering wheel, and he opened his heart to God; he poured out a prayer on my behalf that I couldn't put into words at the time. While he was saying the things that he was asking God to do, I'm telling you, it was darkness. I was thinking, "That will never happen. Lord, I believe. Help my unbelief." And yet two years later, all that he prayed has happened and beyond— things that God did, way more than my friend could think or ask.

That's why David is writing this: "I'm waiting for the God of my salvation. That's part of leaning. I'm going to wait. I'm going to be still. I'm not going to take hold of this myself. Instead, God is the one I'm waiting on." I love that. Wait for your salvation.

VERSES 6–7

Verse 6

Psalm 25:6 begins a little section I'm going to call "seek mercy." Verses 6–7 use the word "remember" three times. David says, "Remember your mercy, O LORD, and your steadfast love."

This is not a plea for God to review his nature as if David is saying, "God, don't forget that you are a merciful God." David is actually asking God to review their personal experience together: "Haven't you done some merciful things for me? Remember your mercies, God. While I wait, I'm remembering your mercies to me, Lord. Remember your *hesed* love, your covenant love, your unimpeachable loyalty, God. Remember what you are like." David calls upon God to do that. He is saying in effect, "You know what you are like, God. And I do too! Your character is what I'm counting on!"

Verse 7

Then David says, "Remember not the sins of my youth or my transgressions." The NIV says "rebellious ways" instead of "transgressions." It's the casting off of allegiance. "I know better than God does. I'm going to do what I want to do my way. I'll do what I want." When you get to a place where you don't know what to do, what is the first thing that can derail your trust in God? The memory of your rebellious ways! Now there's something we're all familiar with: rebellious ways. We may be reluctant to admit it in public, but each of us has a streak of rebellion that is not hidden from God.

We all have rebellious ways. Even the people that we esteem most highly have them. The next person you see has them. The person who faces you in the mirror definitely has them. But when God gets you in a place where you don't know what to do, you're not doing a surface makeover anymore. You're cleaning into the corners. You're saying, "Anything that would hinder the answer to these petitions now has to go." The convenience of secret sins and petty offenses and the nonsense that separates brothers and sisters in Christ all has to go now. "I can have no sin in my life, God, because I have to have the answer from you." When you get to a difficult place under God's providence, you will scour every corner of your soul to remind yourself that God's mercies have surrounded you and that the cleansing river of his grace has flowed into those dry corners. David adds,

> according to your steadfast love remember me,
> for the sake of your goodness, O LORD! (v. 7)

When God gets you to the place where you say, "I don't know what to do," this is part of leaning: *leaning* into God with the kind of trust that is so often neglected even by people in ministry. Flat-out trust him when there is nothing else you can do except *not trust him*, which is the bad plan we follow too often!

VERSES 8-10

Verses 8-9

David transitions in verse 8 a little bit and begins to talk to the congregation. Genuine confession leads to effectively encouraging others. What David wants for himself he wants for others, so he writes,

> Good and upright is the LORD;
> therefore he instructs sinners in the way.
> He leads the humble in what is right,
> and he teaches the humble his way. (vv. 8-9)

He's repeating some of the themes we've already seen.

When I used to sit in seminary, I felt like the teachers intentionally laid it out there and instructed you. You could get it if you wanted it. If you were lazy, you didn't get much. But David refers to more than just-take-it-if-you-want-it instruction. This is God moving toward us and casting us into the way, placing upon us the pressure to get the things that we must get. Like oil down a funnel, like a bowling ball down an alley, like an arrow through a bull's-eye—that's what it feels like in this moment when he casts sinners in the way.

> He leads the humble in what is right,
>   and teaches the humble his way. (v. 9)

Verse 10

Well, does that happen for everybody? No. There is a clause here that creates an exception: "All the paths of the LORD are steadfast love and faithfulness" (v. 10a). *All* the paths—sweet! But then who experiences this steadfast love and faithfulness?

> All the paths of the LORD are steadfast love and faithfulness,
>   for those who keep his covenant and his testimonies. (v. 10)

But sometimes we fail to keep his covenant and testimonies. So implicitly this becomes a renewed determination to be faithful: when I don't know what to do, this is what I'll do. I'm going to receive the discipline that God has given to me. I'm going to obey the correction. I'm going to learn the lesson. I'm going to get to a better place with God's help and commit myself to trust him.

God displays "his steadfast love and faithfulness." We believe that there is a covenant God who, even when he has to step toward me in correction, knows what he is doing. When he steps toward me in that covenant relationship, the way for me to lean is *into* his approach and to *obey* his correction. How critical it is to lean in and embrace what God is doing. To actually trust *and* obey, for there's no other way or path worth going down!

VERSES 11–15

Verse 11

David returns to a theme we've already noticed. Verse 11 is about the hand of God when it is heavy upon you and you cannot carry any extra burdens:

For your name's sake, O LORD,
     pardon my guilt, for it is great.

It is as if he is saying, "I cannot carry this sin anymore, God. I cannot carry this sin and your correction. The weight of my sin and the weight of your correction are too heavy."

But what should you drop? If you were my counselor and I said, "I can't carry the weight of all my sin and God's correction. I'm kind of new to this Christian thing. What should I drop?" you would probably answer that dropping my sin sounds like a good and godly plan! That is what David is saying here when he writes,

For your name's sake, O LORD,
     pardon my guilt.

All this for your name's sake, for the fame of your great name, for your reputation. We know what you're like and what you've said about yourself, and we've experienced it. For your name's sake, O Lord, pardon my guilt. Pardon my guilt for it is great.

Thank God for correction! I am not the person I was five years ago, and I do not want to be that person ever again. Thank God for the correction that brings us to the place where we see the pride and the self-centeredness and the things in our life that injure others and alienate us from the One whom we serve.

For your name's sake, O LORD,
     pardon my guilt, for it is great.

Amen. We need forgiveness. We desperately need God's forgiveness. We need to say, in effect, "I am laying down my sin unreservedly, before you have to pry it from my cold, lifeless hands, God. I'm going to lay it down willingly."

Verse 12

That's a big part of *leaning*. "I need forgiveness, God. I can't go forward the way I am. If I have to go through another trial like this,

I at least want it to be about something different. I want to learn these things." In verses 12–14, David talks about what might be called "choosing covenant." "Who is the man who fears the LORD?" (v. 12a). Fear, of course, is the attitude that seeks a right relationship to the source of fear. If I fear the fire, I don't put my hand in. If I fear the police, I drive the speed limit. The problem in ministry is that we fear the wrong stuff. We fear the loss of our reputation. We dread the failure of our ministry. We dodge the disapproval of others. But all along the One we ought to fear is God! Paul had this nailed: "With me it is a very small thing that I should be judged by you or by any human court" (1 Cor. 4:3).

"Why, Paul? You don't care what people think?"

"Well, sort of. But here's the deal: he who judges me is the Lord."

Maximizing your focus on what God thinks of you will defeat the fear of man quickly.

> Who is this man who fears the LORD?
>> Him will he instruct in the way that he should choose.
> His soul shall abide in well-being. (Ps. 25:12–13a)

Verse 13

"His offspring shall inherit the land" (v. 13b) further states the blessings. Cast in terms of the old covenant, the righteous man who turns from sin establishes his family and heritage, inheriting the land. That's the pattern of how God works.

Verse 14

"The friendship of the LORD is for those who fear him" (v. 14a). Some translations say, "the secret of the LORD" (KJV, NASB). There's an intimacy that comes to those who choose that covenant relationship of fearing God, and "he makes known to them his covenant" (v. 14b). How phenomenal!

Choose covenant. This is covenant theology in the best sense of the word: a person makes the covenant relationship that God offers the great study of their life. That is what God is calling us to, and that is something we have to learn when God takes us through a time when we don't know what to do. How's that going with you? Is God's covenant becoming dearer and deeper to you along the way?

When you go through trials, you learn that the same sun that melts the ice also hardens the clay. You get *better* or you get *bitter* when you choose how you will lean into God's ways. It's true with my wife, Kathy, and me with these trials that we've been through. I'm closer to my wife than I've ever been before. Married twenty-seven years, I'm so thankful for her. But there were critical junctures in the difficult times when we were going to either come together or go apart. Either these events were going to force us into a deeper relationship, or they were going to cause us to separate and be distant from one another.

Thank God that we pursued relationship. And what's true in the horizontal is true in the vertical. So many people who have gone through ministry trials haven't got better. They've become bitter. I remember one of my best friends in college who was so much more gifted than I. He was so capable of serving God. He had a bad first experience in ministry, and he hasn't walked with the Lord for more than two decades. I asked him, "Why don't you want to be a pastor anymore?"

He replied, "Crap treatment for crap pay."

That was his assessment of serving Jesus Christ. How sad that that should happen. But people get bitter, and maybe you're one of those with a big dose of bitter. You need to allow what's happened in ministry to force you deeper into relationship with your covenant-keeping God, not away from it.

Verse 15

The next phrase affirms an expectant outlook:

> My eyes are ever toward the LORD,
>   for he will pluck my feet out of the net. (v. 15)

What a fantastic truth and promise.

My mandate is to show how this passage points toward Jesus, and I do not want to shortchange that task. I have prepared comments on the rest of Psalm 25, but I want to give most of the remainder of the space to my main task. So let me briefly refer to the remaining verses and comment in very speedy fashion before I turn to my main task.

VERSES 16-19

What David says in verses 16–19 is really, "Do you feel me, God? Do you feel what I'm feeling? I need to know, God. You've got me here, and I need to know you feel what I'm feeling."

I'll just read the verses:

> Turn to me and be gracious to me,
> for I am lonely and afflicted.
> The troubles of my heart are enlarged;
> bring me out of my distresses.
> Consider my affliction and my trouble,
> and forgive all my sins.
>
> Consider how many are my foes,
> and with what violent hatred they hate me.

It's all there. "I need to know that you understand what I'm feeling, God. I need to have you connect with me there."

VERSES 20-21

Finally, in verses 20–21, David prays,

> I take refuge in you.
> May integrity and uprightness preserve me
> for I wait for you.

In other words, "I guard my soul. Deliver me. I don't know how long this is going to go on, God, but I'm not going to be able to go another day if you don't keep me."

IS JESUS IN PSALM 25?

Is Jesus in this passage? Is Jesus *ever* in this passage! He *owns* this passage. Jesus is everywhere here. Three thoughts tie this together:

JESUS EMBODIES MY TRUST

Note the frequent repetition in the psalm: "O LORD" (v. 1), "O LORD" (v. 4), "O LORD" (vv. 6, 7, and 11); "is the LORD" (v. 8); "of the LORD" (vv. 10 and 14); "fears the LORD" (v. 12); "toward the LORD" (v. 15). The "LORD," here capitalized ten times, translates *Yahweh*. It is God's covenant name. It was revealed to Moses by the burning bush: "God said to Moses, 'I AM WHO I AM.' And he said, 'Say this to the people of Israel, "I AM has sent me to you"'" (Ex. 3:14). The proper noun is very closely related to the verb "to be": God's name is: I AM WHO I AM. Yahweh is I AM.

Undoubtedly there are limits to what we can understand of the Trinity. But we can see the triune God in Scripture. And in this framework we learn that Jesus is the "I AM." Jesus is Yahweh.

Sometimes the text clearly refers to the Father as Yahweh. For example, Paul says,

Come out from among them
and be separate, says the Lord. . . .
And . . .
I will be a Father to you. (2 Cor. 6:17–18, NKJV)

Sometimes Yahweh is the Father.

Sometimes Yahweh is the Holy Spirit: "We all, with unveiled face, beholding the glory of the Lord, are being transformed into the same image from one degree of glory to another. For this comes from the Lord who is the Spirit" (2 Cor. 3:18).

And every Gospel writer agrees that Jesus himself is also the Lord of the Bible, of the Old Testament. For example:

- Each Gospel includes the saying: "The voice crying in the wilderness, prepare the way of the Lord."

- Isaiah writes, "I saw the Lord . . . high and lifted up" (Isa. 6:1). John 12:39–41 says that Isaiah saw Jesus.
- Numbers 21 says that "the Lord" sent the fiery serpents. Paul says that Christ sent the fiery serpents (1 Cor. 10:9).
- Jesus Christ calls himself Yahweh when he says, "Before Abraham was, I am" (John 8:58). He could have said, "Before Abraham was, I *was*." That in itself would have been scandalous. But he says, "Before Abraham was, I am." To those hearing him, the claim is blasphemous. It would have been except that it's true. Jesus calls himself the "I am."
- John beautifully lays out this thesis in the seven "I am" statements in his Gospel.
- It was also Jesus by the burning bush.
- It was Jesus in the fiery furnace.
- David brought his crushed spirit to Jesus, the One whom the Father was pleased to crush (see Isa. 53:10.) So Jesus Christ is the one whom I trust.

JESUS EXEMPLIFIES MY TRUST

Jesus is my perfect example of trusting God in the midst of betrayal. Jesus embodies the kind of trust we need in the absence of obvious certainties. Jesus exemplifies that kind of trust because his pain was deeper. He experienced fully what we can know only in part.

Can you believe that we worship a God who was betrayed? If we wonder about the impact the betrayal had upon him, we only need to gaze into the flow of the upper room discourse (John 13–17). Not only was Jesus sold cheaply for thirty pieces of silver by "my close friend in whom I trusted" (Ps. 41:9), but while sitting at the table, he knows what is about to happen.

Jesus breaks into the conversation, "One of you will betray me" (Matt. 26:21). *It's the one who's dipping his bread with me right now. Behold my betrayer's hand is on the table. Woe to him by whom the Son of Man is betrayed. One of you will surely betray me. Do it quickly.* How many people, knowing what Jesus knows, do you think would be distracted at the dinner? Jesus is already feeling the crushing weight of the betrayal. Jesus isn't just the one in whom I trust, but he's also the one who exemplifies *how* to trust because his pain is deeper than David's ever was, because his passion is fuller than David's.

Jesus is alone. He pleads for the cup to pass: "My Father, if it be possible, let this cup pass from me; nevertheless, not as I will, but as you will" (Matt. 26:39). What an example of how he processed what God providentially brought him.

One of the verses my mom taught me early was John 18:11. When Jesus is about to leave the garden under arrest after Peter has used his sword, Jesus turns to him and says, "The cup which my Father has given to me, shall I not drink it?" In other words, "What else am I going to do?" Jesus, taking the theme of David's prayer in Psalm 25, takes it to its greatest conclusion of total submission to God the Father.

Jesus embodies my trust. He exemplifies my trust. Finally, he enables my trust.

JESUS ENABLES MY TRUST

Jesus is the one not only upon whom I lean and from whom I learn how to lean. He is also the one at work in me, giving me the *desire to lean*. I'm "prone to wonder, Lord, I feel it. Prone to leave the God I love," but Christ in me is the hope of glory. I am crucified with Christ, nevertheless, I live. He gives me the desire to go through a trial. He keeps my soul so that I'm not lost in bitterness or end up upside-down in the ditch in despair. He enables me to trust.

CONCLUSION

Let me add this pastoral note in closing. We're learning a lot from Psalm 25 and the rest of Scripture. We're exposed to teaching from God's Word. I hope you're being stretched and ministered to. The best way I know how to conclude a message like this is to encourage you to think about it very personally. And the way that I know how to do that is just to invite you to bow your head with me. It is time to lean into what God's Spirit has been speaking to your heart, making David's words your own:

> To you, O LORD, I lift up my soul.
> O my God, in you I trust. (vv. 1–2a)

So if you are carrying a very heavy burden, I want to encourage you right now. Let your humility declare, "I'm not afraid to acknowledge that I'm at a hard place right now. I need the Lord to help me." Jesus himself is here. He is here now, and by his Spirit he can do for you what no one else can do. He can lift that burden that you are carrying. He can give you the oil of gladness for your sorrow. He can give you the capacity to wait upon him for another day, another week. He can carry that burden from you.

5

THE RIGHTEOUS BRANCH

Jeremiah 23:1–8

Conrad Mbewe

In Jeremiah 23:1–8, the prophet says:

"Woe to the shepherds who destroy and scatter the sheep of my pasture!" declares the LORD. Therefore thus says the LORD, the God of Israel, concerning the shepherds who care for my people: "You have scattered my flock and have driven them away, and you have not attended to them. Behold, I will attend to you for your evil deeds, declares the LORD. Then I will gather the remnant of my flock out of all the countries where I have driven them, and I will bring them back to their fold, and they shall be fruitful and multiply. I will set shepherds over them who will care for them, and they shall fear no more, nor be dismayed, neither shall any be missing, declares the LORD.

"Behold, the days are coming, declares the LORD, when I will raise up for David a righteous Branch, and he shall reign as king and deal wisely, and shall execute justice and righteousness in the land. In his days Judah will be saved, and Israel will dwell securely. And this is the name by which he will be called: 'The LORD is our righteousness.'

"Therefore, behold, the days are coming, declares the LORD, when they shall no longer say, 'As the LORD lives who brought up the people of Israel out of the land of Egypt,' but 'As the LORD lives who brought up and led the offspring of the house of Israel out of the north country and out of all the countries where he had driven them.' Then they shall dwell in their own land."[1]

---

[1] All Scripture quotations in this chapter are from the English Standard Version.

Leadership is important. You cannot read a passage like Jeremiah 23:1-8 without realizing afresh that good leadership is vital, especially among the people of God. And it is not just in this passage. Again and again you will find in the Bible that "as the leaders go, so go the people of God." Thankfully, there are blessed exceptions, but sometimes the exceptions are regrettable. For instance, the people of Israel rejected the leadership of godly Samuel. Yet God assured him that he was not really the one being rejected; the people of Israel were essentially rejecting God. However, often you find kings in the Old Testament leading people into sin—sometimes into "great sin," referring to idolatry. This would go on until the judgment of God would fall upon the people.

In fact, as you get close to the end of the Old Testament, even the priests are rebuked for their failure to maintain the honor of God among the people of God. Hence, God told the priests through his prophet Malachi that they were the ones dishonoring his name by accepting blind and crippled animals as sacrifices in his temple.

Yet we must not think of the importance of leadership in purely negative terms. The reverse is equally true. When there was revival among the people of Israel, it first began in the king's palace. As heartfelt repentance took place there, the king would then lead the rest of the nation to acknowledge their sin before God. This often resulted in God having mercy upon the people.

It is this subject of the importance of leadership that occupies the mind of the prophet Jeremiah at this stage in his book. Previously, Jeremiah addressed the nations around Israel, giving them a piece of God's mind. Now, in Jeremiah 23, he turns his attention to the people of Israel and urges upon them the need for persistent, godly, and fruitful leadership, which will bring blessing to them and honor to God.

As we turn our attention to this subject, we need to see that this is an issue that is relevant to us at whatever level of leadership we may be—whether it is in the home, in the church, or in the nation. Indeed, at a conference such as this, many of us are leaders in churches and in various para-church organizations (such as theological colleges). Thus as we go through this message, we ought to pray that God will help us to see how he views leadership in the Lord Jesus Christ so that we may make the necessary adjustments in order to be a cause of blessing wherever we exercise leadership and not a cause of judgment.

THE LORD'S INDICTMENT

God takes seriously the failure of leadership among his people because of its devastating effect upon a people whom he loves dearly. This is what Jeremiah deals with as he addresses the people of God and this is why he begins on a note of scathing condemnation.

> "Woe to the shepherds who destroy and scatter the sheep of my pasture!" declares the LORD. Therefore thus says the LORD, the God of Israel, concerning the shepherds who care for my people: "You have scattered my flock and have driven them away, and you have not attended to them. Behold, I will attend to you for your evil deeds, declares the LORD." (23:1-2)

Who were these shepherds that God was addressing through his prophet? The phrase "shepherd" was often used to refer to kings in Israel. However, by the time Jeremiah was speaking here, he also had in mind the priests and the prophets (see 23:9-14). Every form of leadership in the nation needed to listen very carefully to the message that God had put on his heart. Jeremiah is known as the weeping prophet because he felt deeply the wickedness of the people and the judgment of God upon them. "Both prophets and priests are ungodly," he said (v. 11).

What a terrible time it must have been for the nation of Israel. The very people that were supposed to provide leadership in the ways of godliness and righteousness were in fact the ones steeped in wickedness and sin. This broke Jeremiah's heart. It also brought the wrath of God upon his people. At first sight, verses 1 and 2 sound as if the shepherds were forcefully scattering the sheep away from the Promised Land. But when you read verse 3, it becomes clear that it was God who forcefully scattered them among foreign nations. He put the blame squarely on the leaders because they failed to be godly leaders. Their bad example brought God's judgment upon the whole nation.

One of the greatest indictments of our age is the growing number of church leaders whose lives are a scandal even in the eyes of the world. They drink sin as if it were water and lead their churches into similar wicked lifestyles. You had better make sure that you are not numbered among them in the eyes of God. Your mouth ought to be full of the whole counsel of God so that if the people rebel against you, it is because they are rebelling against God. Your life, too, should be a good role model to the people of God so that by your life they can see what it means to be truly godly.

Take your role as a leader very seriously. If you are not interested in putting a high price tag on leadership, then resign your position before God comes to judge both you and the institution over which you exercise leadership—whether it is your home, your church, or any other institution.

THE LORD'S DETERMINATION

If your leadership among God's covenant people is in perpetual failure, he is determined to move in and correct it because of its devastating effect upon his people. God normally does this by raising a new leadership to lead his people forward. This is very clear from verses 3–4. Notice the way in which the "I will" is so emphatic three times over:

> Then *I will* gather the remnant of my flock out of all the countries where I have driven them, and *I will* bring them back to their fold, and they shall be fruitful and multiply. *I will* set shepherds over them who will care for them, and they shall fear no more, nor be dismayed, neither shall any be missing, declares the LORD.

God is essentially telling the leaders of Israel that if they have failed to do the work he has asked them to do, he will do it himself. He will bring healing and restoration among the people. Isn't that the way God always operates? False prophets who survive on corruption and deceit gain a following for a while. Then without warning, God raises an "Elijah" who leads the people in true revival and godliness. It was the same in the days of the decadent Hophni and Phinehas. They were supposed to be priests in the temple, but they turned it into a den of thieves. From nowhere God raised Samuel to replace them and lead the people into the future.

We can go on. In the midst of the disobedience of King Saul, who refused to listen to Samuel's godly and prophetic counsel, God raised David to lead his people. God's choice of Saul's successor was certainly not the most obvious choice because he was the last person in the family that anyone thought about. It was not until God had rejected all his older brothers that his name was added to the ballot roll. This was the man God chose to replace the king.

This is not merely Old Testament stuff. Christian denominations have arisen that were faithful to God and to his gospel to begin with. But somewhere along the line they have imbibed liberalism and low levels of morality. Although outwardly these denominations are still there, it is clear that the lampstand has long been removed. Yet God never leaves himself without a witness. He raises another church or denomination, sometimes coming from inside the dead one, and this is the vehicle through which the good old gospel continues to be sounded forth to the world. That is how God brings true religion back and blesses his people.

This ought to be a warning to us. If as Christian leaders, you get too comfortable in your positions and indulge in doctrinal or moral compromise, thinking that all will still be well, you are only deceiving yourselves. The God of the universe will not allow his agenda to be hijacked by ungodly and selfish leaders. He will raise others in your place. In fact, he has already raised Another, and it is to this person that we must now turn.

THE LORD'S PROMISE

The ultimate leader of the people of God is a promised king—the Lord Jesus Christ. The whole Bible—from Genesis to Revelation—is about him. In the Old Testament, we catch glimpses of him in the promises that God often made when the situation in the nation of Israel looked dark and bleak. This is precisely what God does here. He says through Jeremiah:

> Behold, the days are coming, declares the LORD, when I will raise up for David a righteous Branch, and he shall reign as king and deal wisely, and shall execute justice and righteousness in the land. In his days Judah will be saved, and Israel will dwell securely, and this is the name by which he will be called: "The LORD is our righteousness." (23:5–6)

This is the promise of the whole Bible. If God were to simply raise human shepherds over his people, sin would always bring about their downfall somewhere along the line. The great promise of God is that he is sending Another to lead. Who is this?

This person is referred to in this passage as a branch, "a righteous Branch." This is a very fascinating phrase. We are to understand the phrase "Branch" as referring to his relationship with David. He is to be from the tree of David. David is the root or the main stem, and growing out of this Davidic kingship is to come another king. In that sense, therefore, this person is someone in David's line.

The branch imagery also has to do with branching out—doing things differently and bringing in a new dimension. It is used in that way in Zechariah 6:12: "And say to him, 'Thus says the LORD of hosts, "Behold, the man whose name is the Branch: for he shall branch out from his place, and he shall build the temple of the LORD."'" So, whoever this person is, he will not merely repeat or do his work as the main stem has done. He will do it differently and will bring his people into a new phase of life. He will branch out.

In which way will this person do things differently? It is by his emphasis on righteousness. This is important because it was a lack of righteousness in the first place that caused God to send his people into captivity. There was unrighteousness in the leadership, which trickled down to the whole nation. So if there is to be a permanent restoration, this king has to provide this missing ingredient—righteousness. Only then will the wrath of God be lifted from the people of God. There is need for someone to satisfy the justice of God in every conceivable way. That person needs to be righteous, and he also has to pay the debt incurred due to the unrighteousness of the people. Only then will God's favor return.

I think that we are now in a position to answer the question, Who is this? Who is this who provides leadership to Israel on the basis of righteousness? You don't need to search very far to realize that there is only one person across the whole of history who answers to this description. It is Jesus of Nazareth. The prophet Isaiah said of him:

> For to us a child is born,
>   to us a son is given;
> and the government shall be upon his shoulder,
>   and his name shall be called
> Wonderful Counselor, Mighty God,
>   Everlasting Father, Prince of Peace.
> Of the increase of his government and of peace
>   there will be no end,
> on the throne of David and over his kingdom,
>   to establish it and to uphold it
> with justice and with righteousness
>   from this time forth and forevermore.
> The zeal of the Lord of hosts will do this. (Isa. 9:6–7)

From this passage we learn a few things about this person. First, he is God. He is described not only as "Wonderful Counselor," but also as "Mighty God." This person, who is to come into this world as a baby, is the infinite and most glorious being that angels have worshiped from all eternity. He is the one through whose hands the universe came into being. He governs all the rolling spheres in the entire universe, and also looks after the minutest details of our lives. He is the one who will ultimately judge the living and the dead.

This is the person spoken about here as the king. He is the person who came into the world as a little baby when Israel was under Roman captivity. Isaiah is telling us here that this person will occupy the office of king. He will deliver his people and lead them. And how shall he do it? It will be through justice and righteousness (v. 7). No mere mortal could provide this. No angel in heaven could do it. Someone needed to completely satisfy the preceptive and the punitive aspects of the law of God through his own righteousness. Thankfully, Isaiah ends this section with the words, "The zeal of the LORD of hosts will do this."

Another passage in Isaiah that helps us to pin down the person referred to in Jeremiah 23 is Isaiah 53. One is tempted to cite the whole chapter, but we will limit ourselves to verse 11.

> Out of the anguish of his soul he shall see and be satisfied;
> by his knowledge shall the righteous one, my servant,
>> make many to be accounted righteous,
>> and he shall bear their iniquities.

From this passage, we learn that this servant king will suffer for his people. It will be out of the anguish of his soul.

Jesus did not simply come as a teacher to teach us a few moral precepts so that we can try and follow the ways of God. He did not even come to simply be a good role model so that by looking at his example we can attempt to live like him. If that were all he did, he would have completely failed in his mission because we are born sinners. We are born with corrupt natures, and the disease is on the inside. No mere outward moral examples can reverse that.

Therefore, Jesus had to suffer and die to carry out the work of deliverance, and hence he said to his disciples, "Now is my soul troubled. And what shall I say? Father, save me from this hour? But for this purpose I have come to this hour. Father, glorify your name" (John 12:27–28). And as he made his way to the cross, he fell on his knees before God in the garden of Gethsemane and pleaded with him. The pleading amounted to something like this: "If there is any other way to achieve this purpose to bring that which is the apple of your eye—your elect people—into your kingdom without me going through this excruciating pain, then please, Father, let this cup pass away from me. And yet not my will but yours be done."

We know the end of the story. God sent an angel to strengthen his Son, and finally he went to the cross. He suffered. He paid the price that no one could ever pay. As Isaiah puts it here,

> The righteous one, my servant,
> [will] make many to be accounted righteous,
> and he shall bear their iniquities.

Jesus paid that price, and three days later God raised him from the dead. He could now go back to the Father and say to him, "Let me have the promised Spirit so that I can send him into the world in order to convict my people and convert them to me. He needs to change their hearts, occupy them, and lead them from rebellion to righteousness. He needs to inspire a new leadership among your people who will truly love you." This is what happened when Jesus returned to heaven after his resurrection. He received the blessed Holy Spirit, whom he has sent into the world.

It must be clear by now that only Jesus of Nazareth fully satisfied the description that Jeremiah gave us of the "righteous Branch." Allow me to point you to one passage in the New Testament that also bears testimony to this fact. Luke wrote that an angel, when announcing the birth of Jesus, said to Mary:

> Do not be afraid, Mary, for you have found favor with God. And behold, you will conceive in your womb and bear a son, and you shall call his name Jesus. He will be great and will be called the Son of the Most High. And the Lord God will give to him the throne of his father David, and he will reign over the

house of Jacob forever, and of his kingdom there will be no end. (Luke 1:30–33)

Again, you cannot miss the aroma in these words of the angel, which you would have smelled from the prophet Jeremiah. "I will raise up for David a righteous Branch, and he shall reign as king" (Jer. 23:5).

Although in our text Jeremiah is primarily concerned with the nation of Israel. When you read the rest of Scripture, it becomes evident that it was not the Jews only who were to benefit from this king. Jesus was to be a blessing to the Gentiles as well. That is the bigger picture. That is why in Psalm 2:8 the Messiah is told,

> Ask of me, and I will make the nations your heritage,
>   and the ends of the earth your possession.

Or, as the apostle Paul puts it in 2 Corinthians 5:18–21, "In Christ, God was reconciling the world to himself."

This is where any hope of true, progressive, sustained, and godly leadership over the people of God lies. It is not on the arm of flesh. If it were, it would fail again and again. Rather, it is based on omnipotence. God himself, in the person of his Son, is moving in, and by the help of his own Spirit he will carry on the work to the very end. Jesus is the center of any hope that we will have godly leadership over the church that will see his people sustained and making progress for time and for all eternity. This is why this passage ends on such a glorious note. Let us turn to this glorious end now.

THE LORD'S DELIVERANCE

God will lead his people through the "righteous Branch" in such a glorious way that it will overshadow even the great exodus from Egypt that Israel experienced under Moses. That is a stupendous claim! Look at the way Jeremiah ends our text. He says:

> Therefore, behold, the days are coming, declares the LORD, when they shall no longer say, "As the LORD lives who brought up the people of Israel out of the land of Egypt," but "As the LORD lives

who brought up and led the offspring of the house of Israel out of the north country and out of all the countries where he had driven them." Then they shall dwell in their own land. (23:7–8)

What is Jeremiah saying here? He is saying that compared to what Jesus will do, the exodus in Moses's day will be like a storm in a teacup. The idea here is not to demean the great exodus, but rather to exalt the work of Christ. The exodus was a great event. Remember the plagues that came one after the other until the mightiest potentate in the known world at that time finally surrendered and allowed the enslaved Israelites to leave Egypt. Remember the way in which Pharaoh changed his mind as soon as the people left, and consequently he got his mighty army to chase after them. We all know that adrenaline-pumping story in which that great army chased this nation of unarmed civilians. Remember the way in which suddenly a great cloud appeared in between the army with all its arsenals and these unarmed people, thus frustrating them because they could not close in on them and capture the people of Israel. Remember the parting of the Red Sea, as two huge walls of water went up into the air and an entire nation walked through the river on dry ground. Remember how, as Pharaoh's army chased them and was now in the middle of the sea, Moses struck the water and it covered the pursuers. Thus the mightiest army on the planet was drowned; it came to nothing. Has there ever been such a deliverance from the beginning of time? It is the kind of stuff that action-packed movies and thrillers try to reproduce.

Jeremiah is now saying that when Jesus has finished his deliverance, this will look like child's play. Which period could Jeremiah be referring to? He is certainly not referring to what happened in the 1940s when Israel became a nation! No, we need to search further than that. We need to scan the New Testament for hints. What deliverance does Jesus bring that can overshadow the great exodus?

One possibility is the deliverance that takes place when a soul gets saved from sin. The Bible pictures it as a coming from death to life. The chains that bound the soul in the darkness and filth of sin are totally shattered. The person experiences a transformation of heart and the peace of sins forgiven. To borrow the words of Charles Wesley,

> Long my imprisoned spirit lay
> Fast bound in sin and nature's night;
> Thine eye diffused a quick'ning ray,
> I woke, the dungeon flamed with light;
> My chains fell off, my heart was free,
> I rose, went forth, and followed thee.[2]

Now, as stupendous as that great deliverance might be, I still think we need to search further. What collective deliverance will make the great exodus pale into insignificance? I can only think of one answer. My mind goes to the day that will "break eternal, bright, and fair," when all the ransomed throng of God will come from east, west, north, and south. When they shall come with singing, and everlasting joy shall be upon their heads. When sin is finally and completely done away with. When there will be no more suffering, no more crying, and no more death. Indeed, my mind goes to that day when Satan himself will receive the final blow at the hands of the Lord Jesus Christ. When we will know what it means to finally worship God with an un-sinning heart and to love him perfectly. When Jesus, our great Shepherd, will himself lead us into eternity. Oh what a glorious day!

Something of this is captured for us in the last book of the Bible.

> After this I looked, and behold, a great multitude that no one could number, from every nation, from all tribes and peoples and languages, standing before the throne and before the Lamb, clothed in white robes, with palm branches in their hands, and crying out with a loud voice, "Salvation belongs to our God who sits on the throne, and to the Lamb!" And all the angels were standing around the throne and around the elders and the four living creatures, and they fell on their faces before the throne

---

[2] Charles Wesley, "And Can It Be?," 1738.

and worshiped God, saying, "Amen! Blessing and glory and wisdom and thanksgiving and honor and power and might be to our God forever and ever! Amen." (Rev. 7:9–12)

Look also at verse 17:

> For the Lamb in the midst of the throne will be their shepherd,
>   and he will guide them to springs of living water,
> and God will wipe away every tear from their eyes.

I think this is it. This is the great deliverance that will completely overshadow what happened in the days of Moses. This great deliverance will happen at the hands of our great king, the Lord Jesus Christ, when he returns to wrap up history.

Very well then, what shall we say in response to all this? Four quick points:

First, those of us who are preachers and elders in the church need to remember that the great Shepherd of the sheep wants us to be true leaders. He wants us to bring his sheep from the far country and be faithful in watching over his flock. Are we doing that?

Second, let us always remember that God has finally walked onto the stage in the person of his Son, the Lord Jesus Christ. We are in a new era, the era of his Spirit. Christ is walking among the lampstands. He is saving and sanctifying his people. He will never fail his elect people. Not one of them will be lost.

Third, is this message speaking to someone who is in the far country and feeling the chains of sin around his ankles? Call upon King Jesus to come and deliver you. He is here and he wants to save you. Stop trying and start trusting in him.

Finally, may your eyes see the faithful man, the King of kings and Lord of lords, who will lead us in the paths of righteousness. May you see the nail prints on his hands and on his feet, the price that he paid for you. May you love him dearly and may you worship him forever. Ultimately, he is the One who will lead us into that great and glorious deliverance. Therefore,

[Let us] stand as children of the promise,
[Let us] fix our eyes on him, our soul's reward,
Till the race is finished and the work is done,
[Let us] walk by faith and not by sight.[3]

Let us do these things looking up to this "righteous Branch," our great God and king, Jesus Christ. Amen.

[3] Adapted from "By Faith," Keith and Kristyn Getty, and Stuart Townend, copyright © 2009 ThankYou Music.

6

YOUTH

Ecclesiastes 11:9–12:8

Matt Chandler

Rejoice, O young man, in your youth, and let your heart cheer you in the days of your youth. Walk in the ways of your heart and the sight of your eyes. But know that for all these things God will bring you into judgment. Remove vexation from your heart, and put away pain from your body, for youth and the dawn of life are vanity. Remember also your Creator in the days of your youth, before the evil days come and the years draw near of which you will say, "I have no pleasure in them"; before the sun and the light and the moon and the stars are darkened and the clouds return after the rain, in the day when the keepers of the house tremble, and the strong men are bent, and the grinders cease because they are few, and those who look through the windows are dimmed, and the doors on the street are shut—when the sound of the grinding is low, and one rises up at the sound of a bird, and all the daughters of song are brought low—they are afraid also of what is high, and terrors are in the way; the almond tree blossoms, the grasshopper drags itself along, and desire fails, because man is going to his eternal home, and the mourners go about the streets—before the silver cord is snapped, or the golden bowl is broken, or the pitcher is shattered at the fountain, or the wheel broken at the cistern, and the dust returns to the earth as it was, and the spirit returns to God who gave it. Vanity of vanities, says the Preacher; all is vanity. (Eccles. 11:9–12:8)[1]

---

[1] All Scripture quotations in this chapter are from the English Standard Version.

WHY I FEEL THE WEIGHT OF THIS TEXT

I preached through the book of Ecclesiastes in 2004, and I feel this particular text—Ecclesiastes 11:9–12:8—for a couple of reasons.

DEATHS AT VILLAGE CHURCH

I pastor a very large church that is young. In the almost nine years I have pastored the Village Church, I have performed one funeral for someone over the age of thirty. I have had dozens and dozens of funerals for twenty-year-olds and under-ten-year-olds. So when you're in that type of environment, you begin to understand that life is a lot quicker than you might think. I am under no illusion that any of us is guaranteed to see thirty years—much less sixty, seventy, or eighty. This time we have, this little sliver, really is a gift from God.

We have had multiple babies at our church die of SIDS. The babies go down for a nap and don't wake up. I remember having to walk into those rooms and feeling like Habakkuk did as the Chaldeans approached:

> I hear, and my body trembles;
> my lips quiver at the sound;
> rottenness enters into my bones;
> my legs tremble beneath me. (Hab. 3:16)

My legs became heavy walking into those environments where there was sorrow upon sorrow upon sorrow. And at the time I didn't see a theological framework that would support the weight of that type of sorrow.

I chose to preach on Ecclesiastes because I wanted to be faithful to the Lord and to the people he had asked me to shepherd by preparing them for the reality of life in a fallen world. And in one of the great mercies of Christ, as I was preparing my people, he was preparing me.

CANCER

So I wake up on Thanksgiving morning, November 26, 2009. I pour myself a cup of coffee and head to the chair that I sit in to read the Word almost every morning. On the way to that chair, my wife, who is preparing some dishes to take to my mother-in-law's home for Thanksgiving, asks me to feed our six-month-old. So I get the bottle and feed little Nora and then put her in her Johnny Jump Up. And I have no memory of what happened after that until I woke up in the hospital.

Apparently, I had a grand mal seizure in front of my children. To this day my daughter will not acknowledge that it was a seizure but asks me if I remember when I was snoring because I was making a weird noise. So God's providence shielded her from what was a terrifying ordeal for our family.

I found out that I had a mass in my right frontal lobe, and that right mass needed to be removed. So there was a lot of drama between that Thursday when I had the seizure and when I had a craniotomy on December 4. A well-meaning member of our church came and looked at the scan and said, "Matt, it looks encapsulated. It looks like you're going to be fine. They'll simply watch this thing. They'll probably put you on some seizure meds, and you'll be fine." So I went into the meeting with the neurosurgeon thinking, "This is nothing. We'll just have to monitor it." I was not prepared to hear, "We're going to have to cut out a large chunk of your brain, and this might end badly for you."

I had walked other people through that kind of bad news hundreds of times, but this was the first time I was on the receiving end of it. I felt like I got punched in the soul. I don't know how else to explain it. I wasn't expecting this.

After the craniotomy, I'm thinking, "OK, they've got it, and I'm going to be fine." But then I start to pick up stuff. If you're a pastor who shepherds your people well and walks them through these types of circumstances, you begin to learn the rules at the hospital. So when I get out of surgery, I'm asking questions about the biopsy, and nobody is answering them. I've played this game enough to know that's not good. If they say, "Why don't you get stronger and then we'll talk?" that's bad.

They sat me down on December 15 and said, "The brain tumor is malignant. You have Stage 3 anaplastic oligodendroglioma. It's not encapsulated, and we weren't able to remove all of it. You've got about two to three years to live. That's the average." That sent me and the family reeling. It wasn't long, though, until we landed on what is tried and true: the firm foundation that God doesn't drive an ambulance—this didn't surprise or shock God.

I want to be honest: I'm not wearing a cape. I didn't hear that news from the doctor and immediately respond, "Well, I'm on a firm foundation." That's not how it worked. If that is how it went down in your life, then you have been shown greater grace than I was shown, because the first couple of days were tough.

So when I read Ecclesiastes 11:9–12:8, I feel it. And don't go super-holy on me and say, "Well, you should feel *all* the texts." Well, yes and amen. But I *feel* this one. It creates heat, fire, and angst in me.

Some of you will not be back for the next TGC conference. You think you will. Everybody knows that anyone *can* get that call that changes everything, but nobody thinks that she is getting the call. Yes, your children can die in accidents. Yes, your spouse can become terminally ill. Yes, this can happen to you. But nobody thinks it's coming to him. Pastoral experience almost trains us that it comes to others.

So when I read this text today, its weight, thickness, and pain are a beautiful thing. When I first read through Ecclesiastes and felt the Spirit leading me to preach through the book, I felt that the writer needed a hug. I was thinking, "Man, somebody hug him. Life is not this dark."

THE POINT OF ECCLESIASTES 11:9-12:8

The passage starts out in a way that makes everyone say, "Yes, hallelujah! Amen!" Even the most pagan people would love that first part: follow your heart and whatever your eyes see. Who doesn't want that? Do you know anyone who would have a problem with that? No. Some might say, "Wow, that's in the Bible? Let's go!" But just about the time the writer has got you, he adds, "But don't forget you're going to be judged for all that. You've got to die and stand in front of God. So just don't forget that in your partying."

> Rejoice, O young man, in your youth, and let your heart cheer you in the days of your youth. Walk in the ways of your heart and the sight of your eyes. But know that for all these things God will bring you into judgment. (11:9)

It started so beautifully, and now he's gone dark on us: "Remove vexation from your heart, and put away pain from your body, for youth and the dawn of life are vanity" (11:10).

There are a lot of problems in Ecclesiastes 11:9–12:8. If we just sum them up, the author is saying, "Hey, enjoy your youth. Enjoy your passion. But here's the deal: you're going to be judged for that. And oh, by the way, life's going to go by quickly, and there's going to come a day when you hate that you woke up. And you're going to die. But guess what? Remember that judgment I told you about? It'll be time. So you get to die young and be judged, or you get to hate life and eventually die and then be judged. Good luck. It's all vanity." See what I'm saying? You just want to hug him. You just want to go, "Come here, man."

IMPERATIVES

So you've got a problem in this text, and I think it can be solved by looking at the imperatives in this text. The imperatives lead us to Christ.

REJOICE

Human beings have a rejoicing problem, but it's not that they don't rejoice. It's that they rejoice on the surface. Everyone we know rejoices. You do not know a man or woman who is not an expert at rejoicing. It's just that they are broken in how they rejoice and what they rejoice in.

When Paul in Romans 1 begins to unpack what's wrong with humanity and how the wrath of God is being revealed against mankind, the problem is not that we rejoice but rather what we rejoice in. We rejoice in what? Creation. Not the Creator. In essence we say, "Isn't creation lovely? Look at how spectacular creation is. Look at how amazing creation is." Our rejoicing is shallow because it doesn't roll up into who created what we're rejoicing in. We don't get deep enough in our rejoicing.

And what does Paul say next? People believe a lie over the truth of God (Rom. 1:25). What's the lie? This fallen nature in us believes that we're smarter than God. I've never met anyone who will say that, but I've met hundreds of people who live like that: "I'm smarter than God." God reacts to people who believe the lie over the truth of God. Paul paints the picture of homosexuality, with a man saying, "Forget the woman. I'll take myself." And the woman says, "Forget the man. I'll take myself." And once again people are rejoicing in the wrong thing. "I am smart enough to pull this off. I can do this."

And what's the last problem in Romans 1:28? They did not "acknowledge God." You see this constantly. It's basketball season, and a guy that's seven feet tall does a dance after he dunks. It's just shameful. Any time Shaq jammed the ball and did that thing he did, I was like, "Hit a free throw, brother. Then celebrate." But if you're 7'1" and you dunk the ball, that's like me putting on my shoes. I shouldn't be able to dance or celebrate that. If we think about it, the preborn Shaq didn't rap on the uterus wall and request, "I'd like to be 7'1" and athletic." He was born. "But he worked hard." Okay, but I can work hard, and I can't do that. He was uniquely wired and gifted by God to bring glory to God, and when he tampers with that, he makes himself a blasphemer. When he takes what God gave him for the purpose of glorifying God and uses it to glorify himself, he blasphemes.

I'm from Dallas, home of the largest cult in America. It's the largest church with the most expensive church building you've ever seen. Some men in our church swear to me that they can't read or study well, but they can tell me the name of the third-string running back for the Dallas Cowboys and how many yards he rushed for his junior year of high school. That's rejoicing in football. That's celebrating football.

We don't have a problem in rejoicing. You don't know anyone who doesn't excel at rejoicing. The problem is not in the rejoicing. It's how we rejoice and that we don't get *underneath* what we're rejoicing in to give credit to where credit is due. This leads us to the second imperative:

REMEMBER YOUR CREATOR

The second imperative beats like a drum in this text: *Remember also your Creator* in the days of your youth. *Remember also your Creator* before the evil days come. *Remember, remember, remember, remember, remember your Creator.*

The question we must answer is this: Is there a way of remembering that redeems how we rejoice and fixes the brokenness in how we rejoice?

Throughout the Old Testament this gospel rhythm is established: the Old Testament calls God's people to remember several things about the nature and character of God.

Remember Who God Is

"Remember your Creator" means "Remember that I am God." Through the Prophets and the Law, God constantly says, "I am God. I am the Creator. I started this, and I'll finish this. This was my idea. I did this." And it shows up beautifully in the wisdom literature.

I love Job 38:1–13. It's a terrifyingly beautiful passage. I've asked a lot of questions, and I'm grateful that God hasn't answered me like this:

Then the LORD answered Job out of the whirlwind and said:

"Who is this that darkens counsel by words without knowledge?
Dress for action like a man;
     I will question you, and you make it known to me.

"Where were you when I laid the foundation of the earth?
     Tell me, if you have understanding.
Who determined its measurements—surely you know!
     Or who stretched the line upon it?
On what were its bases sunk,
     or who laid its cornerstone,
when the morning stars sang together
     and all the sons of God shouted for joy?

"Or who shut in the sea with doors
     when it burst out from the womb,
when I made clouds its garment
     and thick darkness its swaddling band,
and prescribed limits for it
     and set bars and doors,
and said, 'Thus far shall you come, and no farther,
     and here shall your proud waves be stayed'?

"Have you commanded the morning since your days began,
     and caused the dawn to know its place,
that it might take hold of the skirts of the earth,
     and the wicked be shaken out of it?" (Job 38:1–13)

And later there's a pause like Job's got an answer: ". . . no."

You also see reminders in moments of worship, like Psalm 147:4:

He determines the number of the stars;
     he gives to all of them their names.

"Remember that I am God. I'm not you. I'm God. I do what you can't. I started this. I'm driving this. I'm beyond you."

Habakkuk is very similar to Job. Habakkuk asks God, "Why

are you putting up with injustice?" And God replies, "I'm not putting up with injustice. I'm sending the Chaldeans to punish my people." Habakkuk responds, "No, you can't come to us in judgment like that because the Chaldeans are more wicked than we are, and you surely won't use really wicked people to judge less wicked people." But God replies, in effect, "Oh, I'm coming. And if you think I'll delay, just wait for it. Remember that I am God."

Remember What God Has Done

God constantly calls people back to remember: "Look, I have accomplished much around you, for you, in you." Here are just two examples.

First, the establishment of the Passover feast: "This day shall be for you a memorial day, and you shall keep it as a feast to the LORD; throughout your generations, as a statute forever, you shall keep it as a feast" (Ex. 12:14). This is a call to remember: "You're going to get together, and you're going to remember that you were slaves and that I freed you. You didn't free yourselves. I freed you. You didn't get yourself out of Egypt. I did. I sent the plagues. I showed my power and authority over the created order. I killed Pharaoh's men. I got you across the Red Sea. I spared your sons. Remember that I am God and that I have delivered you and called you and fulfilled my promises to your ancestors."

Or again, when Israel passes over the Jordan River:

And Joshua said to them, "Pass on before the ark of the LORD your God into the midst of the Jordan, and take up each of you a stone upon his shoulder, according to the number of the tribes of the people of Israel, that this may be a sign among you. When your children ask in time to come, 'What do those stones mean to you?' then you shall tell them that the waters of the Jordan were cut off before the ark of the covenant of the LORD. When it passed over the Jordan, the waters of the Jordan were cut off. So these stones shall be to the people of Israel a memorial forever." (Josh. 4:5–7)

In other words, "Remember what I've done. Don't forget that I delivered you. Don't forget that I didn't abandon you. Don't forget that I am faithful and that I have acted on your behalf."

And there's one more component to this theme in the Old Testament. God adds, "And I'm not doing this because you're awesome." That's what we like to think. We won't say that, but many of us think it. We think that things will go well for us because we're "faithful." But God's message since day one is this: "I'm going do this because *I* am awesome, because *I* am spectacular. Let me show you how spectacular I am. I'm using you. Watch my power flow through you. I'm letting you play in what I'm doing, but it is ultimately about me. Don't forget. I'm faithful. I don't abandon my people."

Remember God's Commands

Remember God's commands, and remember that they are about leading his people into life. The commands of God in Scripture are about lining people up with how he designed the universe to work. God's commands don't rob you of joy but lead you into it. At the Village Church, I try to make that clear for people who don't have a lot of religious background or who have bought into the lie that God is in the heavens with a thunderbolt waiting to light someone up simply for smiling.

A question that people get tired of me asking is, "How's that working for you? So you're smarter than God when it comes to sex. How's that working for you?" I don't think you have to be sharp to see this. You can be a dull blade and look at our culture and conclude, "Man, we're a mess when it comes to sex. We have not figured it out. We're having tons of it, and it's not working." So we're trying to figure out better techniques at doing it because if having it doesn't satisfy, then maybe doing it better will. When you go to the store, look at any magazine you want, and on the cover—it doesn't matter what it is, it could be *Auto Trader*—will be a little line about "how to make her engine rev" or whatever.

It's just ridiculous. So I constantly come back to the question, "Is it working?" If that's how you view sex and freedom, does it satisfy? At the Village Church, I regularly hear testimonies about how that view of sex leads to devastation, heartbreak, pain, disease, sorrow, loss. But God's not taking away enjoyment; he's giving it.

DEUTERONOMY 6:6–9

> And these words that I command you today shall be on your heart. You shall teach them diligently to your children, and shall talk of them when you sit in your house, and when you walk by the way, and when you lie down, and when you rise. You shall bind them as a sign on your hand, and they shall be as frontlets between your eyes. You shall write them on the doorposts of your house and on your gates. (Deut. 6:6–9)

God says, "Remember my law because if you remember my law and practice my law you will see how great and beautiful and amazing I am and how much I'm for you and how much I love you and how much I am trying to lead you into how I designed things to work for the glory of my name and your ultimate joy."

NUMBERS 15:39–40

When God speaks to his people, he is rarely seeker-sensitive.

> And it shall be a tassel for you to look at and remember all the commandments of the LORD, to do them, not to follow after your own heart and your own eyes, which you are inclined to whore after. So you shall remember and do all my commandments, and be holy to your God. (Num. 15:39–40)

I just love that: "Hey, whores, listen to me. I'm already on your frontlets, hands, doorposts, gates. Now put tassels on your clothes." The Old Testament establishes this gospel rhythm. This idea of remembering rightly redeems our rejoicing.

LUKE 22:19

In the New Testament, Jesus, God in the flesh, shows up on the scene (cf. John 5 and Luke 24) and points back to the Old Testament and says, "See, that was me." At his final Passover meal, Jesus says that the blood is the blood of the new covenant. "And he took bread, and when he had given thanks, he broke it and gave it to them, saying, 'This is my body, which is given for you. Do this in remembrance of me'" (Luke 22:19). We got into that gospel rhythm in the Old Testament, and it doesn't get broken in the New Testament. You're still in that rhythm.

Remember! Remembering rightly will redeem rejoicing. Your rejoicing is broken, so you must remember rightly, and then you'll rejoice rightly. You'll get underneath the surface, and you will rejoice in what you should rejoice in rather than staying on the surface and robbing yourself of joy and God of glory.

1 CORINTHIANS 11:26

Paul takes this and runs like an Olympic sprinter: "For as often as you eat this bread and drink the cup, you proclaim the Lord's death until he comes" (1 Cor. 11:26). Paul points back to the institution of the Lord's Supper as a remembrance of the cross of Christ: "Don't forget what Jesus told you not to forget."

One of my favorite aspects of Paul's ministry and one that I think we need to hear over and over again is that he loved to preach the gospel, not only in a frontier setting—he gets a lot of credit for preaching the gospel in a frontier setting, and rightly so—but he also constantly preaches the gospel to Christians. Over and over again he proclaims to people what they already know because we are all prone to forget. We are prone to wander and drift. So Paul wants to preach the gospel to people who know it because even gospel people are prone to forget the gospel or at some level just assume it, which can create a lot of pain and heartbreak. He says:

I do not want you to be unaware, brothers, that I have often intended to come to you (but thus far have been prevented), in

order that I may reap some harvest among you as well as among
the rest of the Gentiles. I am under obligation both to Greeks and
to barbarians, both to the wise and to the foolish. So I am eager
to preach the gospel to you also who are in Rome. (Rom. 1:13–15)

This is an interesting text because Paul says, "I want you to
know that I want to reap some harvest among you, my *brothers*."
So he is not referring to justification, to salvation, but rather to
playing a role in their continued maturation into their knowledge
of Jesus Christ.

Some of you who have more foolish people than wise at your
churches should take comfort in verse 14. I've picked up on some
things as I have gotten to know pastors. For instance:

1. Nobody wants the ministry of Moses. We love Moses; we just
   don't want his ministry—wandering around in the desert for
   forty years with grumbling and complaining people and then
   dying right before it gets better. Moses saw the Promised Land
   and could say, "There it is!" But God said, "No, you don't get
   to go. I'm killing you up here, and Joshua's taking them in."
2. Everybody loves Pauline theology, but nobody wants Pauline
   pain.

1 CORINTHIANS 15:1–4

This is a watershed right here:

Now I would remind you, brothers, of the gospel I preached to
you, which you received, in which you stand, and by which you
are being saved, if you hold fast to the word I preached to you—
unless you believed in vain.

For I delivered to you as of first importance what I also
received: that Christ died for our sins in accordance with the
Scriptures, that he was buried, that he was raised on the third
day in accordance with the Scriptures. (1 Cor. 15:1–4)

Paul is addressing brothers here too—not pagans. They have
already received this gospel. That's in the past. And these believers

are still standing in the gospel; they are being saved by this gospel, and they will be saved by this gospel. The gospel of Christ is what saves us, sustains us, and brings us safely home. We do not move on from the gospel. If you preach it in such a way that you give the impression that Christians should move beyond the gospel, then you will remove from them the very lifeline of a Spirit-empowered relationship with Jesus.

Paul warns:

> I am astonished that you are so quickly deserting him who called you in the grace of Christ and are turning to a different gospel— not that there is another one, but there are some who trouble you and want to distort the gospel of Christ. But even if we or an angel from heaven should preach to you a gospel contrary to the one we preached to you, let him be accursed. As we have said before, so now I say again: If anyone is preaching to you a gospel contrary to the one you received, let him be accursed. (Gal. 1:6–9)

Then you've got that spectacular, Mount Everest–like section of texts in Galatians 2:20–3:5, where Paul (showing that he is a preacher) says, "I'd like to learn just one thing from you." And then he asks something like six questions, saying in effect: "Did you come into the kingdom because you did something, or did you come into the kingdom because the Spirit of God made you alive in Christ? After being saved that way, are you now being perfected by the law?" He's already told them: "I have been crucified with Christ. It is no longer I who live, but Christ who lives in me. And the life I now live in the flesh I live by faith in the Son of God, who loved me and gave himself for me" (Gal. 2:20). And there is Ephesians 1–2, where Paul gives a cosmic-level view of the gospel. It's spectacular.

PHILIPPIANS 1:12–17

I have never met a man as free as Paul. You can't touch him. If you say, "I'm gonna kill you, Paul," he says, "All right! Time to go home."

If you say, "We're gonna let you live," he comes back, "All right; to live is Christ."

You say, "Okay, we are going to beat you," and he says, "Well, you know, that's sharing in the sufferings of Christ. I welcome that." If, "We'll put you in prison," no problem: "I'll convert all your guards and most of the prisoners."

Paul is untouchable. How did he get like that? He kept going back to the gospel over and over again. That's what he says in Philippians 1:12–17. He says, "You know, I'm here in prison, but that's fine. That has emboldened others for the gospel. So I'm here and able to share the gospel here. Everything drives the gospel forward."

Colossians 3

Paul always wants to clearly set up the gospel before he gets into specific applications: "Now because of the gospel, do this." So there are these great turn texts in Paul's letters. Colossians 1 is a great christological beginning; it breaks down who he is and what he's done and what God is accomplishing. And Colossians 3 swings it by beginning, "If then you have been raised with Christ . . ." In other words, "If you've been baptized into this, if you're a believer, then let's look at marriage, children, church, life. But if you don't get the gospel, we can't have these conversations. Because if I preach these conversations before I preach the gospel, you get hung up on trying to accomplish what only Christ in you can accomplish."

So now we come back to our main text.

Ecclesiastes 11

When we remember what we've been commanded to remember, then our rejoicing is redeemed because we'll move past the surface and get underneath it. So let's look back on some of the things we're supposed to rejoice in according to Ecclesiastes 11. "Rejoice, O young man, in your youth, and let your heart cheer you in the days of your youth. Walk in the ways of your heart and the sight of your eyes" (v. 9).

If I can rejoice—having remembered what Christ has done, having remembered what he has purchased for me, being spiritually aware of what Christ has done for me in his perfect life on the cross and in his resurrection—in my youth, in my physical strength, I'm not rejoicing merely in my youth and my physical strength. I'm rejoicing that God in his mercy has granted it to me. And because of the grace of Christ, God has freed me up in my youth to serve him faithfully. See, I get underneath it. I don't rejoice in being young and having a strong, healthy body. I rejoice in being redeemed. Youthful strength, zeal, and passion are redeemed so that I might rejoice that I'm here.

Control is an illusion. You eat all the spinach you want. You can get your Pilates workout on. You can get in the gym and pump weights and run. You can be as careful as you want with that, but it's not going to save you. Should we wisely steward our physical bodies? Absolutely. But at the end of the day, my rejoicing isn't that I'm young and strong, because that can be taken from me in a second. That can be ripped from any one of you in a second. What can't be ripped from me is that in this moment God has given me strength and energy to make much of him. So I don't rejoice that I'm young. I rejoice that in my youth he has opened my eyes to how beautiful and spectacular he is. In the energy of my youth, I get to make much of him.

Ecclesiastes 11:9 also says that we should rejoice in the desires of our heart and eyes. So here is how you "get underneath" the desires of your heart and eyes. I have a beautiful wife whom I love very much, and the last year and a half has made that even more spectacular to me. I try to help her around the house and be a good daddy and love and lead my home with all the grace the Lord gives me. But when someone cuts out a big portion of your brain, there's a period of time that you're down. And you don't get to do those things. Add to that the amount of steroids you're on. Suddenly I just cried a lot. Where I had been strong and able to run things in the home, I just cried. I couldn't hold myself together. I was so ready to be off the steroids not because I was raging but because I couldn't stop crying. We'd go to a movie, and there'd be a commercial for St. Jude's Hospital, and I'd start sobbing. In that season I had nothing to give, no way to lead my girl.

There's something underneath that: Ephesians 5. It's like that day of epiphany when a guy goes from thinking that girls are gross to thinking he has to have one. That's not some sort of weird biological hormonal thing. God's driving that. God's painting a picture. So underneath, the heart I have for my wife is this beautiful picture of what God has done for me in Christ. And when there are issues (i.e., when my wife acts up)—and the only people who think that marriage isn't difficult are people who aren't married or who just got married; there are definitely seasons when you irritate your spouse and come to impasses; there are moments when you need help—we get this great lesson. If we're seeing and remembering who Jesus is and remembering this great analogy of the wedding supper of the Lamb and of being the bride of Christ, we start to see underneath our marriage. I am not just rejoicing in Lauren, but I get underneath that and rejoice that God has made a covenant with me. God is not leaving me—ever. And that's not built on my performance or how well I please him but rather on who his Son is.

I love being a daddy. If there is something greater than that outside of being a child of God—I love it. I love what kids say. I love the innocence of their hearts. And I love how often, if you'll pay attention, God is teaching you about himself in them—whether that is from how they trust or from our oldest starting to walk. I believe that a young child walking really isn't so much a decision of the will as much as it is some weird physiological thing that happens. So if you've got kids, they start to crawl. And they start to rock back and forth. And then they start to scoot along the side of something. And then what do they do? They let it go, right? They kind of awkwardly hobble. And then because God has created children with giant heads and small bodies, the head falls forward. Now science is involved: now you've got momentum. So the kid at this point has two choices: take a step or die. So the kid steps, and now we're moving. Now we're in physics. Step, step, step, and then what happens? Fall. But what do we do? We freak out like the kid just got a football scholarship: "He's walking!" We're calling people. We're tweeting. We're setting the kid back up and taking pictures. We freak out: our kid took two steps and fell on the ground.

We have a young church with a lot of young children, and we have never seen a father watch his kid take three steps and fall and say, "Idiot. Are you serious? Baby, this is your side of the family because we walk in my family. We walk!" You don't say that. How crazy would that be? No, you celebrate the steps, don't you?

So I'm watching my oldest do this, and I'm just blown away that she's walking. She's fifteen months, and I'm thinking, "She's going to drive before she walks." But here's the picture I got watching Audrey fumble her way into walking: Step, step, fall. And there's this great rejoicing in the steps. And we scoop her back up and say, "Go on again." And "Get the camera! We're going to film this." And we'd just watch her and wait for her to do it again. And we'd celebrate again. But it never bothered us that she would fall. We knew that she was starting to walk and that she would get better and better at it until she was running. Since we knew that it was going to end with strong walking and running and climbing, the falls didn't bother us. As I'm watching my kid learn that, I'm blown away at grace. That's what I'm seeing. Celebrate your steps.

Because so many of us believe the gospel, we don't remember the gospel well enough. The litmus test of whether you understand the gospel is what you do when you fail. Do you run from God and go clean yourself up a little bit before you come back into the throne room? Or do you approach the throne of grace with confidence? If you don't approach the throne of grace with confidence, you don't understand the gospel. You think you can get yourself clean enough to stay in the club.

It's not you only at your worst that God has a problem with. It's you at your best. It's when you nail it that you're filthy before the Lord. When you get up and have your quiet time and get into Edwards and you're trying to learn to play the acoustic guitar so you can lead worship before you preach and you share the gospel with your neighbor and you go to the gym and talk to some guy who is bench-pressing and you use the bench press as an entry to a gospel narrative, and it's brilliant, lights out—it's on that day that you are offensive to God without Jesus. The idea that the Reformed community hasn't bought into the idea of earning favor is foolish. I meet young and old men all the time who are still trying to earn what has been freely given.

REMEMBERING IN A WAY THAT LEADS TO RIGHT REJOICING

In our jobs and callings, we begin to get underneath them when we understand what Jesus Christ has done. When we remember what Jesus has done, that takes us underneath that surface level of rejoicing. It takes us out of the kiddy pool and into the deep end of the pool, where joy can be ever expanding and the glory of God can shine, and we can be sustained in that rejoicing.

This is not just a mind-set. This is not just, "Let me change how I think about things so that I can remember correctly and thereby fix my rejoicing issue." That's not how it works. How do we get into remembering in a way that leads to rejoicing correctly?

HAVE A REGENERATE HEART

First, you need a regenerate heart. You need to be born again. You're a much better pastor when you're saved than when you're not. You're a much better pastor when you understand the message not just in your head but having been transformed by the Holy Spirit of God—not conformed to a mere pattern of religion.

My fear for some of you is that as you grew up in church, you learned early on that by saying certain things and acting in certain ways you got power and credibility and applause. You've learned to play the game so well that by being Reformed and making much of Jesus, much is made of you. And in the end you have not been converted. You've just been conformed to a pattern of religion. You haven't been transformed by the Holy Spirit of God. You must war with that. I feel no guilt in wanting you to question whether you know him, love him, serve him.

MEDITATE ON THE GOSPEL

Second, you need to constantly mediate on the gospel of Jesus Christ. After all of these years of trying to faithfully serve the Lord by the power of the Spirit sealed inside of me by the grace of God, I still have to preach the gospel to myself.

Just a few months ago, I was preaching near my hometown, and I had a little bit of a break. So I thought it'd be a good idea to go see some of the houses in the area that I lived in and take some pictures and show them to my kids. There was one where I got saved right before my eighteenth birthday. I drove into town and saw a field where I got into a fight with a kid named Shawn in front of a whole bunch of people. I'm not a fair-fight kind of guy. I don't have that kind of physique. I had to take a cheap shot and keep wailing until somebody broke it up. So some bad, dark things happened in that field to the point where Shawn, to this day, if God hasn't saved him, would flush at the mention of my name.

Then I drove by one of the houses we lived in, and I took a picture. And I was immediately filled with memories of things that occurred in that house. I felt shame. Then I drove by Jimmy Herford's house and remembered his sixteenth birthday party, and I was immediately filled with shame.

So I got back in my car and drove back to preach. And the entire drive back, I'm being accused—and not by the Holy Spirit because when the Holy Spirit accuses, it's sweet. When the Spirit convicts, there's a sweetness to it. Not so when it's the lies of the Enemy. So I'm driving, and I'm fighting with myself: "Oh, you're going to talk to them about what a man of God you are and what a man of God they're supposed to be? That's what you're going to say? You're going to point guys toward the gospel? What do you think Shawn thinks about your gospel? What do you think Holly thinks about your gospel? What do you think most of your friends from high school think about your gospel?" I'm going to preach on believing the gospel, and I'm having to wrestle with myself to believe it myself.

It was somewhere in the middle of that wrestling that the promise of the covenant and the blood of Jesus Christ and the knowledge of Scripture really defeated what was the work of the Enemy because I got to say, "No, *that* Matt Chandler is dead. *He* should never say anything about Jesus. Good thing Jesus killed him on the cross. Good thing that the new Matt Chandler is holy and righteous, and not because *he* is but because it was granted to him." Now, all of the sudden, I get to walk in gospel power.

Do not assume the gospel. It must be explicit, and it must constantly be explicit. If you assume it, then all people will hear is moralistic therapeutic deism: "Do this. Don't do that. Go here. Don't go there." They will not understand that their righteousness is blood-bought. Don't assume it.

We baptize tons of twenty-year-olds who say to us in our baptism class, "I grew up in church and never heard the gospel." We always want to press on that because sometimes you just don't have ears to hear. So we ask, "Did you take any notes when you were in youth group?" "Yeah." "Go back and look at your notes, and tell me that you didn't hear the gospel." And a lot of them come back and say, "Yeah, I heard the gospel. I guess I just didn't have ears to hear." But there are an amazing number of young men and women who were told, "Don't drink beer. Don't have sex. Don't listen to secular music." Should we call young people to holiness? Absolutely. Is holiness possible outside of the working of the Holy Spirit to regenerate us? No. Even if they didn't have sex, didn't touch beer, and didn't listen to anything but Sandi Patty, does that in the end redeem them? No. They're just nerdy lost kids.

Make the gospel explicit. Preach it week in and week out. "Well, people will get tired of hearing it." I've been doing it for nine years, and they don't get tired of hearing it.

WALK BY THE SPIRIT

Third, walk by the Spirit and not by the flesh (Gal. 5:16). I want to stay deeply tuned in to my affections—like when I no longer marvel, when I'm no longer overwhelmed, when I'm no longer stirred up and enflamed that God in his mercy saved me. I didn't save myself, he saved me. I had a plan for me, and it wasn't his plan. He came and got me; I wasn't looking for it. I moved from California to Texas and "happened" to have a locker next to a guy in football who came up to me and said, "Hey, I need to talk to you about Jesus. When do you want to do that?" Not, "Hey, would you like to hear about Jesus?" It wasn't an option; he was going to tell me. But he did let me pick the place: "Where do you want to have the conversation. It's happening, but where do you want to have it?"

So I want to stay dialed in to the fact that God came and saved me. I want remembering to lead to rejoicing, and when that's not taking place, I want to be nervous and get around other brothers who can help me work through why I'm not marveling at what should be more spectacular than anything else in the universe.

CONCLUSION

Some of you are young and feel young. Some of you are at your cruising altitude for a while. Some of you are on the descent, and for some of you the tray tables are stowed, the chair back is up, and you don't wonder if you'll be here for the next conference. When I said that earlier, you were thinking, "Probably, that's me. I probably won't be here." So we're all over the map.

But here's the reality. I need you to hear me, and I don't know if you will. We are right now several hours closer to standing in front of our great Father and Judge than we were when we walked in. I'm wondering how you're doing at rejoicing. That's the question on my heart for you. Are you rejoicing well? Are you remembering in such a way that you're getting underneath how most men rejoice? Are you rejoicing in what God has done for you in Christ? Are you rejoicing in what Colossians calls those shadows? Are you looking at your marriage and going, "Isn't the Father spectacular?" Are you looking at your children, your job, your life, the nuances of everyday life, and are they stirring up a passion within you for God's mercy? Or is your rejoicing hollow? Is it shallow? Are you in the kiddy pool? Or are you swimming in the ocean?

My hope for you is that you know the deep waters, that the Holy Spirit would invade in simple acts every day to draw your attention and focus to who he is and what he has done. That is the firm foundation that is unshakeable. That's how you become a man or woman who is unmoved. That's how you glory in crazy circumstances. When you hear "cancer" or experience loss, you mourn, yes, but you are very quick to say, "Yes, Lord, accomplish what you want to accomplish." There is a confidence that comes when remembering redeems rejoicing that's simply not there when you rejoice in your youth because you're young. Or you rejoice in your money because you have money. Or you rejoice in your wife because you have one and she likes you for now. Or you rejoice in your children because they're healthy and doing what you say. Or you rejoice in the nice car or house that you have.

All that can be taken from you. You're not free. But when remembering leads to rejoicing, you'll be a man or woman unshaken. And that's my hope for you.

7

GOD'S GREAT HEART OF LOVE TOWARD HIS OWN

Zephaniah

Mike Bullmore

In John Bunyan's famous book *The Pilgrim's Progress*, right from the outset of the book, we are introduced to a man who is deeply troubled and who is also very conspicuously reading from a book. The man, named Christian, explains to his family his distress in reading that their city is doomed to burn with fire from heaven, but his family offers no real comfort. During one of his many walks in the fields, while reading his book Christian bursts out, "What shall I do to be saved?"

A man named Evangelist appears and asks, "Why are you crying out?" The story continues:

> He [Christian] answered, "Sir, I understand from reading the book in my hand that I am condemned to die and after that to come to judgment. I am not willing to do the first, nor able to do the second."
>
> Then Evangelist asked, "Why are you not willing to die, since this life is attended with so many evils?"
>
> The man answered, "Because I am afraid that this burden that is on my back will sink me lower than the grave, and I shall fall into Hell."
>
> "And, sir," continued the man, "if I am not ready to die, then I am not prepared to go to judgment and from there to execution. Thinking about these things distresses me greatly."

Then Evangelist said, "If this is your condition, why are you standing still?"

The man responded, "Because I do not know where to go."

Then Evangelist gave him a parchment and unrolled it so that the man could read, "Flee from the wrath to come."

When he had read it, the man looked at Evangelist very carefully and said, "Which way should I run?"

Then Evangelist, pointing with his finger to a very wide field asked, "Do you see the distant narrow gate?"

"No," the man replied.

Then Evangelist asked, "Do you see the distant shining light?"

"I think I do," the man answered.

Then Evangelist said, "Keep that light in your eye, and go up directly toward it, and soon you will see the narrow gate. And when you finally come to the gate, knock and you will be told what to do."[1]

Now I can imagine someone reading that and saying, "Clearly the problem is with that book that he's reading. What he needs to do is stop reading that book. Just put the book down and move on. That will relieve his distress."

Christian is saying, "I understand from reading the book in my hand that I am condemned to die and after that to come to judgment."

Condemned to die!? Come to judgment!? Christian, just put this book down and pick up something a little bit more positive, something that will make you feel better about life and about your-self. I mean, why would you want to read that when there are magazines about celebrities, romance novels, best sellers, and all sorts of fluffy entertaining things to occupy your attention?

Why would you read that book? Unless . . .

Unless what that book says is really true—unless what that book says is what is really going to happen, while all the other stuff is designed and calculated to distract you and keep you in a make-

[1]John Bunyan, *The Pilgrim's Progress: From This World to That Which Is to Come*, ed. C. J. Lovik (Wheaton, IL: Crossway, 2009), 20–22.

believe world. Why would you read such a book unless it is the one thing speaking about reality, and your only hope is in paying attention to it and doing what that book tells you?

Well, the book that Christian is reading is of course the Bible—God's Word. And this book of Zephaniah could very easily be the place in God's Word from which Christian is reading. This book of Zephaniah is this book in miniature. Most of the prophets are like that. In fact, what we're trying to say with this entire conference is that the entire Old Testament is like that.

The Old Testament is pregnant with the message of the Bible. In other words, we could say the Old Testament is pregnant with the gospel of Jesus Christ. It is round with the gospel; it is great with gospel.

Now, granted, in the earlier stages of salvation history, in the earlier stages of progressive revelation, the gospel is more difficult to detect. But as salvation history progresses, the shape and the promise of the gospel become more evident.

So as we read through the Old Testament, either in its entirety or in its pieces, it is increasingly easy to detect the specific contours and the specific content of the gospel. And that is certainly the case when we get to the prophet Zephaniah.

The gospel is here in utero, but with all its essential parts in place. It begins with a sober assessment, a sober announcement of the condition of mankind sinning against God. It then pronounces God's righteous judgment on sinful mankind.

But in the midst of the pronouncement of judgment with all its darkness and all of its gloom and distress and anguish, there comes shining through like a bright ray of light, a word of hope from God: the word of the good news of salvation from God, good news for sinful man under the judgment of God. Despite God's righteous judgment, because of God's mercy there is hope for sinners like us. And the picture Zephaniah paints of where that all ends up is almost beyond belief. What Zephaniah tells us is that God has provided salvation, and not just as an escape from God's judgment, but as an entrance into God's very joy.

I don't think it is too simplistic to say that Zephaniah proceeds in these three steps:

- Step 1: There appears to be no hope—God's judgment is rightly against all mankind.
- Step 2: There appears a glimmer of hope—a word of hope is spoken.
- Step 3: That glimmer of hope bursts into a great and glorious rejoicing at the consummation of the salvation of God's people.

So let's follow this prophet Zephaniah as he takes these steps. And let's hear "the word of the LORD that came to Zephaniah the son of Cushi, son of Gedaliah, son of Amariah, son of Hezekiah, in the days of Josiah the son of Amon, king of Judah."

STEP 1:
THERE APPEARS TO BE NO HOPE

Zephaniah 1:2–4a says:

> "I will [entirely] sweep away everything
>   from the face of the earth," declares the LORD.
> "I will sweep away man and beast;
>   I will sweep away the birds of the heavens
>   and the fish of the sea,
> and the rubble with the wicked.
>   I will cut off mankind
>   from the face of the earth," declares the LORD.
> "I will stretch out my hand against Judah
>   and against all the inhabitants of Jerusalem."[2]

These opening verses of Zephaniah have got to be some of the most dramatic and silencing opening verses of any book in the Bible. God says, "I will utterly sweep away everything from the face of the earth." Why? It is because of how the people of

---

[2] All Scripture quotations in this chapter are from the English Standard Version.

Judah and the people of other nations were posturing themselves toward God.

Let's see how they were posturing themselves toward God. In verse 5 we read about

> those who bow down on the roofs
>   to the host of the heavens,
> those who bow down and swear to the LORD
>   and yet swear by Milcom.

It looks like the people of Judah were trying to cover all their bases; they were succumbing to cultural pressure. "How can your God be the only god?" the people around them were saying.

And so they became good religious pluralists. They bowed down to the sun and stars like those around them. They swore allegiance to the Ammonite God Milcom. And oh, they included the Lord, too, so as to cover all their bases and not offend anyone.

And God was very offended.

God had said ever so clearly. "You shall worship the one true God and him only." Worshiping God *and* something else is not worshiping God at all. They weren't worshiping God. They were patronizing God.

Then look at verse 6:

> Those who have turned back from following the LORD,
>   who do not seek the LORD or inquire of him . . .

They were pretending, at least in some ways, to believe in God and yet were living as practical atheists without reference to him at all.

We were made for God. We were made to be in a dependent relationship with God. We were made to trust in him with all our hearts and lean not on our own understanding. In all our ways we are to acknowledge God and seek him and inquire of him.

We are to say in every situation, "God, I want to think about this situation the way you think about this situation. I want to feel about this situation the way you feel about this situation, so that I can act and live in this situation in a way that is pleasing to you—how I spend my time, how I spend my money, how I relate to those around me." But the people Zephaniah is addressing "do not seek the LORD or inquire of him" at all.

Then look at verse 12.

> At that time I will search Jerusalem with lamps,
>   and I will punish the men
> who are complacent,
>   those who say in their hearts,
> "The LORD will not do good,
>   nor will he do ill."

Not only were they patronizing God and not only were they neglecting God, but they were trivializing God, marginalizing God, saying, "He's not really a factor in the equation of our lives. He really doesn't matter one way or the other. What matters is the bottom line of my business. What matters is my reputation in the community. What matters is my comfort at home. God? If he exists, he's not involved. He doesn't really need to be taken into consideration."

And we see all this posture of heart captured in 3:2. Speaking of Judah and Jerusalem, the prophet says:

> She listens to no voice;
>   she accepts no correction.
> She does not trust in the LORD;
>   she does not draw near to her God.

The people of Judah are proud and self-sufficient. They think they don't need input from anybody, not even God. And so Zephaniah, the prophet of God, with a word from God, sent by God, comes and says to them:

> The great day of the LORD is near,
>   near and hastening fast;
> the sound of the day of the LORD is bitter;

the mighty man cries aloud there.
A day of wrath is that day,
    a day of distress and anguish,
a day of ruin and devastation,
    a day of darkness and gloom,
a day of clouds and thick darkness,
    a day of trumpet blast and battle cry
against the fortified cities
    and against the lofty battlements. (1:14–16)

A day of wrath is coming. Think of what Christian was reading in his book. God is absolutely just.

He does no injustice;
every morning he shows forth his justice. (3:5)

God is absolutely just and absolutely holy, so when he sees this rebellion and this pride and this blatant idolatry, he is (there is no other way to say it) angry, full of wrath—and he will judge.

You know this happened to Judah. God delivered on this promise. A matter of years after Zephaniah's prophecy, Jerusalem was utterly destroyed. The Babylonians came. First they attacked and invaded the city and carried away many exiles. Then they came back and destroyed the city—tore down its walls and demolished the great temple Solomon had built. Zephaniah probably witnessed that with his own eyes.

But that now-historical day of God's judgment on Judah was just a foretaste of the great and terrible day of the Lord that is coming on all unrepentant humanity. What it will be like is described in Scripture. It will be a day of anguish and wailing like nothing mankind has seen. All mankind will be laid bare before the heat of the fire of God's wrath. Those who think they are safe in their great cities will be absolutely overwhelmed by God.

God is holy and in his holiness he punishes sin. He will bring justice. If there is no turning, he will bring judgment. He will set things right.

All of this judgment is due to one thing. We see it there in the middle of 1:17. "Because they have sinned against the LORD." This announcement of judgment is in this book for a reason. The very first truth about God to be denied—at least as recorded in Scripture—is the doctrine of God's judgment. Do you remember what the serpent said to Eve? "You will not surely die" (Gen. 3:4).

We want to think our neglect of God is insignificant; we want to think that our sins are minor, that they are small and that they do not matter and will have no consequences, so that we are free to do whatever we want. But God says judgment is coming. "I will bring distress on mankind." And this is for all peoples. Look at Zephaniah 3:8:

> "Therefore wait for me," declares the LORD,
>   "for the day when I rise up to seize the prey.
> For my decision is to gather nations,
>   to assemble kingdoms,
> to pour out upon them my indignation,
>   all my burning anger;
> for in the fire of my jealousy
>   all the earth shall be consumed."

This applies to everybody. God is the greatest reality in the universe—and not just the universe as a whole but in every person's universe—in your personal world.

So the question is, Where have you put God in your universe? Are you neglecting God? Trusting yourself? Are you patronizing God? Saying, "Okay, I'll go to church." Are you trivializing God, saying, "Oh, he doesn't care what I do or how I live." There will be judgment for all who have neglected or patronized or trivialized God. Destruction is coming—fearful, burning, wailing. I don't know how else to say it.

And verse 18 of chapter 1 makes it very clear that neither your riches nor your wealth, neither your accomplishments nor anything else will be able to save you on that day. There will be nothing to hide behind. We tell our children regularly that there is coming a day when they have to stand alone before God. They can't stand behind Mom and Dad. Everything will be laid bare.

And God's Word is plain. All the earth, all mankind is under that judgment.

If step 1 doesn't register for you, if it doesn't strike you as true, you will never even bother to listen to step 2 and step 3. You'll just say, "Stop reading that book with all its talk of judgment." And if you never hear and respond to steps 2 and 3, you will be lost forever.

And if you are a believer, the Bible is regularly calling you to consider how it was for you and how it still would be for you apart from the grace of God: "lost and without hope in this world."

That's step 1: there appears to be no hope. All mankind is under the just and certain judgment of God.

STEP 2:
THERE APPEARS A GLIMMER OF HOPE

Do you remember in *The Pilgrim's Progress* when Evangelist pointed across a wide field and asked Christian, "Do you see the distant narrow wicket gate?" And Christian said, "No." And Evangelist asked, "Do you see the distant shining light?" And Christian said, "I think I do." And Evangelist said, "Keep that light in your eye." Just a glimmer, but still a light amid all of this dark, thick, gloom.

Now look at Zephaniah 2:1–3:

Gather together, yes, gather,
   O shameless nation, [notice this repetition—this relentless
      repetition]
before the decree takes effect
   —before the day passes away like chaff—
before there comes upon you
   the burning anger of the LORD,
before there comes upon you
   the day of the anger of the LORD.
Seek the LORD, all you humble of the land,
   who do his just commands;

seek righteousness; seek humility;
　　perhaps you may be hidden
　　on the day of the anger of the LORD.

It seems like such a tiny little glimmer. "Perhaps you may be hidden." Perhaps you might find refuge. And then as if to heighten and emphasize the narrowness of that ray of hope, the little glimmer is again surrounded by judgment all around, and I mean literally all around.

Earlier in chapter 1 God's words of judgment were particularly aimed at the people of Judah, but now in chapter 2 that judgment is directed to the nations all around Judah as well.

- Judgment will come on the Philistines to the west (v. 5).
- Judgment will come on Moab and Ammon to the east (v. 8).
- Judgment will come on Cush to the south (v. 12).
- Judgment will come on Assyria to the north (v. 13).

And as we read those words of judgment in chapter 2 and are at least a little bit familiar with the political geography of the ancient Middle East, we begin to see what God is doing. He is saying, "Yes I am the Lord of all nations and all nations are accountable to me."

But God is also saying, "Listen, Judah, any way you turn, you will run into judgment. There is no place for you to flee for safety. No way for you to turn. No one to whom to turn."

That is, except one: only a little glimmer, only a narrow gate, only one place to turn for refuge and salvation. And that is to turn to God himself. "Seek the LORD." There alone is your hope. Seek the Lord.

Perhaps you've heard this said before, "The glory of the gospel is this. The One from whom we need to be saved is the very One who saves us." It's true.

When you realize that you really do stand guilty before a holy, righteous God, when that happens, when that registers for you, when you realize that monumental and fundamental truth, right then there is a temptation in every human heart to turn to all sorts of other refuges, other remedies. "I'll go back to church, God." "I'll stop doing such and such, God. I'll clean up my act." "I'll be better, God."

Listen, there is no hope there. There is only one place to turn, and that is to God himself, who in his mercy provided salvation through Jesus Christ to all who would turn to him and say, "Lord, be merciful to me a sinner. Save me." That's not some magic formula. No, that is the humbling of your heart. It is humbly turning to Christ and taking refuge in his death for your sins.

It is God's intent to rescue and redeem for himself a people, a remnant. Look at 3:12. After speaking about his judgment against the proud he says:

> But I will leave in your midst
>   a people humble and lowly.
> They shall seek refuge in the name of the LORD. (v. 12)

Here is hope! And for those who turn there for refuge, step 3 is what then happens.

STEP 3:
THE GLIMMER OF HOPE BURSTS INTO REJOICING

God does save. That glimmer of hope will burst into a great and glorious rejoicing at the consummation of the salvation of God's own.

Remember, salvation is not just an escape from God's judgment. Even more, it is an entrance into God's joy. Look again in chapter 3, verses 14–17.

> Sing aloud, O daughter of Zion;
>   shout, O Israel!
> Rejoice and exult with all your heart,
>   O daughter of Jerusalem!
> The LORD has taken away the judgments against you;
>   he has cleared away your enemies.
> The King of Israel, the LORD, is in your midst;
>   you shall never again fear evil.

On that day it shall be said to Jerusalem:
"Fear not, O Zion;
    let not your hands grow weak.
The LORD your God is in your midst,
    a mighty one who will save;
he will rejoice over you with gladness;
    he will quiet you by his love;
he will exult over you with loud singing."

Those in view are those who have received God's salvation by turning to the Lord, by seeking refuge in his name—and it is clear from Scripture that these blessings are not just for the nation of Israel, but are for all of those who through faith in Christ are inheritors of the promises. Remember what Paul says in Galatians 3:29: "If you are Christ's, then you are Abraham's offspring"—Israel— "heirs according to the promise."

Those who have received God's salvation, notice here, are called to rejoice, to sing—and this isn't some kind of tame singing. They are called to sing and shout and rejoice with all their hearts.

And given what's been done for you, you have every reason to rejoice with all your heart. No experience here on earth that might cause us to shout and rejoice comes anywhere close to what those who have put their trust in Christ will experience. And when that is brought to full consummation, you won't be able *not* to rejoice with all your heart.

In this lifetime we grasp the significance of our salvation only partially, only vaguely. Now we see through a glass darkly, but then we shall see him face to face. The full realization of what we have and what God has done will break upon us. And what is it that we will realize then? We will fully realize that there is no judgment for us—no judgment at all.

Look at Zephaniah 3:15: "The LORD has taken away the judgments against you." What a beautiful statement of the heart of the gospel right here in this little obscure Old Testament, so-called "minor" prophet. What a beautiful statement of justification. The Lord has taken away the judgments against us.

When he endured the wrath of God for us on the cross, Christ drained the cup of God's wrath bone dry. In him the fullness of the wrath of God was poured out. If we are in Christ, all the judgment for our sins was paid, so there remains no judgment for us. Do the math. And so we sing,

> The judgments of your holy law
> With me can have nothing to do.
> My Savior's obedience and blood
> Hide all my transgressions from view.[3]

So too we sing, "*All* my sins are washed away." And we sing,

> My sin, oh, the bliss of this glorious thought!
> My sin, not in part but the whole,
> Is nailed to the cross and I bear it no more.[4]

And then we say, "There is therefore now no condemnation for those who are in Christ Jesus" (Rom. 8:1). For those who are in Christ, the Lord has taken away the judgments against them. So, there's no judgment. We will realize the full significance of that then.

And second, we'll realize the amazing experience of being in God's very presence. Look again at the middle of Zephaniah 3:15. The king of Israel, the Lord is in your midst. You shall never again fear evil. On that day it shall be said to Jerusalem,

> Fear not, O Zion;
>   let not your hands grow weak.
> The LORD your God is in your midst,
>   a mighty one who will save. (vv. 16–17)

And third, we will realize that there will no longer be any reason for fear of any kind. I wonder what that's going to be like. No reason for and no experience of fear. Because there is no judgment

---

[3] Augustus M. Toplady, "A Debtor to Mercy," 1771, modified.
[4] Horatio G. Spafford, "It Is Well with My Soul," 1873.

and your all-powerful king is right there in your midst, you shall never again fear evil. On that day it shall be said to Jerusalem:

> Fear not, O Zion;
>> let not your hands grow weak.
> The LORD your God is in your midst,
>> a mighty one who will save.

Zephaniah wants the people of God to see these things, to get a glimpse of them so that by getting at least a little glimpse of them we might be strengthened and encouraged as we follow God now.

But clearly, what Zephaniah marvels at the most, and what he holds up for us to marvel at, is the amazing prospect of God rejoicing in love over us on that day. Having rescued and redeemed a people for his very own, when that work of redemption is done and all whom God has saved—people from every tribe and every tongue and every nation—are gathered, God declares,

> At that time I will bring you in,
>> at that time when I gather you together. (v. 20)

When that time comes, what will happen? Will he look out over us and somehow be disappointed in the fruit of his saving work? Will he look at us and think, "Well, given what I had to work with . . . well, it is what it is." No, he tells us—now don't miss this, for he put it in this book, so he wants us to know—that on that day he will rejoice over us with gladness. He will exult over us with loud singing.

He will have perfectly completed his purpose to make us spotless and without blemish. So his rejoicing in his work will be right. Do not miss the unrestrained intensity of God's passion. He will rejoice. He will exult. His singing will be loud. There is an intensity of passion in the heart of God. He will say: "I don't do this reluctantly. I'm not doing this begrudgingly." There is no constraint involved here at all. As the prophet Isaiah says,

As the bridegroom rejoices over the bride,
so shall your God rejoice over you. (Isa. 62:5)

Not long ago I was in a conversation with a woman from our church. I wanted to thank her and commend her for her influence in our church, but as I was doing that she kind of grabbed the reins of the conversation and began to commend my wife to me. Now please do not misunderstand; my purpose here is not to call attention to my wife. I just want to illustrate something. This woman was describing my wife to me as she reflected on her conversation with Beverly a few days before. She was describing my wife to me in glowing terms. It wasn't a token thing; she went on for quite a while and I made absolutely no attempt to stop her. And all the while, as I listened, my heart was full of joy. There was a great gladness in my heart. I wasn't the least envious: I was delighting, out of love for my wife, in what was being said. My heart was full of joy.

If you are in Christ, that's how God feels about you.

As the bridegroom rejoices over the bride,
so shall your God rejoice over you.

Only a million times more.

And one day, Zephaniah tells us, one day when he "brings us in," when he "gathers us together," that rejoicing that God holds in his heart for you will break forth and you will experience the most incredible thing you've ever experienced. I don't care what you've experienced in this lifetime. You might have stood on the summits of the highest mountains of all seven continents. This is going to make all of the moving and thrilling and delightful experiences of this life seem like nothing. God will greatly rejoice over you.

Yes, you will rejoice, but even greater than your joy will be God's joy. Listen to Spurgeon:

Believer, you are happy when God blesses you, but not as happy as God is! You are glad when you are pardoned, but he who pardons you is more glad! The prodigal son come back to his home was very happy to see his father—but not as delighted as his father was to see him. The father's heart was more full of joy, because his heart was larger than his son's.[5]

God's heart is bigger than ours. Because of Christ, God's heart is completely for us and his heart is large. This book of Zephaniah is here to let us know that—as hard as it is for us to fathom this—when God's work of redemption is done and we are gathered with him, with all of his own, when he has brought us in, God himself will stand and will break forth in singing and will rejoice over us with all his heart.

He will sing, "I have betrothed you to me forever. I have betrothed you to me in righteousness and justice, in steadfast love and mercy. You are mine" (cf. Hos. 2:19). And we will say, "And you are our God."

He will sing, "I have cleansed you from all guilt and I have forgiven all your sin, and you shall be a joy and a praise and a glory to me" (cf. Jer. 33:8–9). And we will say, "Who is a pardoning God like you?"

He will sing, "I will make you dwell in safety, and you will be my people and I will be your God, and I will rejoice in doing you good with all my heart and soul" (cf. Jer. 32:37–38, 41). And we will say, "Whom have we in heaven but you?"

And he will sing over us again and again, "You are mine, you are mine, you are mine." And he will rejoice over us with gladness and exult over us with loud singing. And we will be "radiant over the goodness of the LORD"; and we will feast on his abundance, and we will be satisfied in his love (Jer. 31:12–14).

Let me conclude with something of a footnote of pastoral encouragement. You know we have conversations about the exact content of the gospel. What is the gospel? What must it include when we share it? What must it include when we preach it? I be-

---

[5] C. H. Spurgeon, "The Whole-Heartedness of God in Blessing His People," Sermon 2036 of *Metropolitan Tabernacle Pulpit*, July 29, 1888, accessed http://www.spurgeongems.org/vols34-36 /chs2036.pdf (p. 5).

lieve these have been very helpful and clarifying conversations, and I'm thankful to the men who have led us in them. But may I say this morning that our thoughts of the gospel, our preaching of the gospel, our personal treasuring of the gospel should always include this consummation, including the vision of God's joy over his people, the end to which it's all moving. Certainly we can't leave out the aim, the goal, and the consummation of it all. This is the whole point: being with God and experiencing his joy—to his rightful glory. This is the grand point of it all, isn't it? And this, I believe, is the great contribution of Zephaniah, this vision of the consummation of the redeeming work of God in Christ.

Sometimes I'm afraid we forget to speak about this great consummation. But it needs to be spoken. It doesn't work as an unstated assumption. There is something existentially very unsatisfying about that. It must be spoken. And that's exactly what Zephaniah does. And I am eager that our preaching of the gospel, both our preaching to others and our preaching to ourselves, not leave this out.

May we as God's people see it and hear it and treasure it until it fills our hearts with eagerness and our souls with an anticipation of all this joy. To Christ's glory. Amen.

8

GETTING EXCITED ABOUT MELCHIZEDEK

Psalm 110

D. A. Carson

Hear the word of God, Psalm 110, the Old Testament chapter quoted most often in the New Testament:

Of David. A psalm.

The LORD says to my lord:

"Sit at my right hand
    until I make your enemies
    a footstool for your feet."

The LORD will extend your mighty scepter from Zion, saying,
    "Rule in the midst of your enemies!"
Your troops will be willing
    on your day of battle.
Arrayed in holy splendor,
    your young men will come to you
    like dew from the morning's womb.

The LORD has sworn
    and will not change his mind:
"You are a priest forever,
    in the order of Melchizedek."

The Lord is at your right hand;
    he will crush kings on the day of his wrath.
He will judge the nations, heaping up the dead
    and crushing the rulers of the whole earth.
He will drink from a brook along the way,
    and so he will lift his head high.[1]

Most of the controlling themes in the Bible do not resonate very well with the dominant secular culture of the West—and for that matter with many other cultures as well. Think through many of the controlling categories:

1. Covenant
2. Priest
3. Sacrifice
4. Blood offering
5. Passover
6. Messiah
7. King
8. Day of Atonement
9. Year of Jubilee

I guarantee you that there are not a lot of people on the streets of Chicago asking, "I wonder when the Year of Jubilee is coming."

We speak of "King Jesus." When Jesus began to minister, he did not announce the dawning of the Republic of God. The last king we had in America was King George III, and he didn't turn out too well. If instead we come from a Commonwealth country and still nurture a lot of respect for Her Majesty Queen Elizabeth II, nevertheless we recognize that she is a *constitutional* monarch; she has very little real power. But the king in the Bible is not a constitutional monarch. So even a notion that is common enough—like king—means something very different in our culture. It has different resonances.

Again, most people on the streets of Chicago are not thinking, "I hope my high priest is up-to-date on his repentance when he offers that blood sacrifice this year. I really feel the need for atone-

---

[1] All Scripture quotations in this chapter are from the New International Version.

ment. I hope he does a good job in the Most Holy Place." People in our world do not think in those terms at all. Of course, some exposure to priesthood is found among Roman Catholics and Episcopalians, but that is pretty far removed from Levitical priesthood or Melchizedekian priesthood.

Yet precisely because he is both king and priest, the figure of Melchizedek turns out to be one of the most instructive figures in the entire Bible for helping us put our Bibles together. He helps us see clearly who Jesus is.

This address is going to involve some hard mental work, but God has put these things together in the Bible in this way not only for our instruction but also for our good.

Melchizedek shows up only two times in the Old Testament: once in Genesis 14 and then again in Psalm 110. Then he shows up in only one book in the New Testament: Hebrews. Yet he turns out to be utterly revolutionary in opening our eyes to the glories of our Savior.

PSALM 110

We begin with Psalm 110. Here we must ask two questions. The first may sound a little out of place.

WHO WROTE PSALM 110?

You may think, "Don, for goodness' sakes, stay out of the classroom." In the classroom you discuss a lot of things about who wrote what and when and why. We burden our students with these things, and they have to pass exams on them. "Just get us to the text," some may mutter. Certainly in some instances, it doesn't make a lot of difference who wrote what. But in this instance it makes a huge difference, so we must ask and answer the question, Who wrote this Psalm?

In most of our English Bibles, there is a superscription before the psalm that occurs after the bold-faced title **Psalm 110** and prior to verse 1. It may occur in italics and a smaller font, *Of David. A psalm*, or something of that order. But there are many contemporary commentators who do not think that David wrote this psalm. They think that such superscriptions were introduced to the psalms later.

Suppose that David did not write this psalm. How would you read it?

The Lord says to my lord:

"Sit at my right hand
   until I make your enemies
   a footstool for your feet." (v. 1)

If David did not write it, it sounds as if "the Lord" (i.e., Yahweh)—the living, covenant God—is speaking to, apparently, "my lord" the king (i.e., the king of Israel). So the author of the psalm would not be the king of Israel but a courtier—someone in the king's court. Many psalms appear to be written by a courtier. So if we get rid of the superscription, then a courtier wrote this psalm. In that case, this psalm sounds a lot like Psalm 2 and others that are royal and Davidic and promise conquest over the enemies.

But the superscription will not go away. Of the various manuscripts that have come down to us, not one leaves it out. In our printed Bibles, we have a little font for "Of David. A psalm" or something similar; we have a bigger font for "Psalm 110." But of course, they did not have distinctive fonts in the days before printing presses. What is remarkable is that in all the manuscripts that have come down to us, this superscription is part of the psalm. It is not an add-on that was introduced later; it was counted as part of the psalm.

But if these arguments were not enough, in this instance we rely on the words of the Lord Jesus himself. For the validity of one of Christ's arguments turns on the Davidic authorship of this psalm (Matt. 22:44–45; Mark 12:36–37).

While Jesus was teaching in the temple courts, he asked, "Why do the teachers of the law say that the Messiah is the son of David? David himself, speaking by the Holy Spirit, declared:

" 'The Lord said to my Lord:
   "Sit at my right hand
   until I put your enemies
   under your feet." '

David himself calls him 'Lord.' How then can he be his son?"
The large crowd listened to him with delight. (Mark 12:35–37)

The point is that if David the king has written this (i.e., the writer is not a courtier addressing the king), then to whom does "my Lord" refer? It can't be David because he is not talking about himself. So Jesus draws the conclusion that David must be talking to someone who is greater than David himself. But to whom does King David say "my Lord"—apart from Yahweh himself? Therefore, this must be the anticipated Messiah. And Jesus himself takes it that way.

Jesus essentially says, "You are used to thinking of the Messiah as the son of David. And in one sense, of course, he *is* the son of David." But if the Messiah is *merely* the son of David, then in the order of thinking of the day, that would make the Messiah ultimately inferior to David. We do not understand that well in the West because we think that the really important people are the young people. But in many cultures of the world, the really important people are the older people. So I am always of less honor than my father, who is of less honor than his father, who is of less honor than his father, and so on. That means that David's son cannot be greater than David; he must be inferior. If you think of Jesus as David's son and nothing more, your Jesus is too small. For David himself anticipates this person coming by speaking of him as "my Lord." He says, "The Lord [i.e., Yahweh] said to my Lord [i.e., the Messiah]": he is picturing messiahship that escapes mere sonship to David, as important as that sonship is in fulfilling the promise of the Davidic line to conceive of a Messiah who, though David's son, is also David's Lord.

So this psalm is talking about the Messiah, about the one who was to come, about Jesus. David wrote it about a thousand years before Christ. That date, as we'll see, is important.

WHAT DOES PSALM 110 SAY?

The second question we must ask is, What does this psalm say? If you look at it closely, it is divided into two oracles, and commentary follows each oracle.

> Oracle 1 = verse 1
>   Commentary = verses 2–3
> Oracle 2 = verse 4
>   Commentary = verses 5–7

Oracle 1 (Ps. 110:1)

"The Lord says to my lord" (v. 1). The exact words pick up an expression that is very common in the prophets, especially Jeremiah and Ezekiel. Directly rendered, it reads, "Yahweh's utterance to my lord." This is a very common prophetic declaration. This is a way of saying that David here functions as a prophet. David declares what God is declaring to the one David himself refers to as "my lord." And David says that Yahweh says to him,

> Sit at my right hand
>   until I make your enemies
>   a footstool for your feet. (v. 1)

Do you have any idea how often the New Testament quotes or alludes to that little expression "Sit at my right hand"? It comes up again and again. Below are some of the inferences that New Testament writers draw from this little expression. In them Yahweh, the great covenant God, is addressing the Messiah. What do we infer from this?

1. He is greater than David. "For David did not ascend to heaven, and yet he said . . ." (Acts 2:34).
2. He is greater than angels. "To which of the angels did God ever say . . . ?" (Heb. 1:13). There is no other mediating person who sits at the right hand of God.

3. He is exalted to God's side. As one author has put it, "God exalted him as emphatically as man rejected him." "God exalted him to his own right hand" (Acts 5:30–31).
4. His session (i.e., his being seated at God's right hand) grounds his intercession for us. "Christ Jesus . . . is at the right hand of God and is also interceding for us" (Rom. 8:34; cf. Acts 5:31).
5. His session signals the completion of his sacrifice. "Day after day every priest stands and performs his religious duties; again and again he offers the same sacrifices, which can never take away sins. But when this priest [i.e., Jesus] had offered for all time one sacrifice for sins, he sat down at the right hand of God" (Heb. 10:11–12). It signals that Jesus's cross-work is utterly finished. The sacrifice of Jesus does not have to be repeated.
6. He awaits the ultimate conquest and surrender of his enemies. "He sat down at the right hand of God, and since that time he waits for his enemies to be made his footstool" (Heb. 10:12–13).

These are six theological inferences about the Messiah that are drawn from this one little phrase in Psalm 110:1: "Sit at my right hand."

The words "until I make your enemies a footstool for your feet" envisage the Messiah's conquest, his active, controlling confrontation of the enemy. And God himself is going to do it now that the sacrifice has been paid.

Commentary (Ps. 110:2–3)

All of God's people will be so transformed that they will serve willingly in the Messiah's army:

> The Lord will extend your mighty scepter from Zion, saying,
> "Rule in the midst of your enemies!" (v. 2)

This is an astonishing passage. It is not saying simply that God confronts the enemies all by himself. Somehow he is calling together the Messiah's army and making them willing to do his bidding. This anticipates the transformation that comes in the gospel.

> Your troops will be willing
>   on your day of battle. (v. 3)

God's people become willing on the day of his battle. When he wants to use them, he makes them willing; he transforms them.[2] This tells us something about the strange nature of this army and this military service. The same sort of overtone occurs in a different context—a more military context—in Judges 5:2:

> When the princes in Israel take the lead,
>   when the people willingly offer themselves—
>   praise the Lord!

So here in Judges we have a picture of the rulers of Israel operating in justice and taking the lead against the enemies, and the people willingly follow them. In Psalm 110, the Messiah—at God's right hand—displays his power and so transforms his people that they willingly follow him and constitute the Lord's army and push the enemies back. That is the vision.

That last half of verse 3 can be translated in several different ways. I won't go through the options here. But it sounds to me as if this envisages a splendid army of the young arising freshly, silently, and in holy splendor to do their Master's bidding:

> Arrayed in holy splendor,
>   your young men will come to you
>   like dew from the morning's womb. (v. 3)

Oracle 2 (Ps. 110:4)

The second oracle still addresses the Messiah.

> The Lord has sworn
>   and will not change his mind:
> "You are a priest forever,
>   in the order of Melchizedek." (v. 4)

---

[2] That is part of what we mean, is it not, by regeneration and conversion, so that our hearts now want to do his bidding when at one time we wanted to do only our own.

We will return to this verse, but on first reading it is staggeringly out of place. After all, according to the law of Moses, which had been given some centuries earlier, a priest could not be a king, and a king could not be a priest. God himself destroyed the first king of the united monarchy, Saul, because Saul tried to mingle those two roles. David certainly understood that. So what is David doing here envisaging a Messiah who is transparently the king—the king from Jerusalem, the king from David's line—now being a priest, regardless of the order? It really does seem very strange.

And what is Melchizedek doing here? What is going on in David's mind as he writes this? We will come back to this in a moment, but look first at the commentary that follows.

Commentary (Ps. 110:5-7)

Verses 5–7 give you another surprise. Once you have seen the two oracles and the first commentary, then you expect a pattern:

Oracle 1 (v. 1) about the king
    Commentary (vv. 2–3) about the king's rule
Oracle 2 (v. 4) about the priest
    Commentary (vv. 5–7) about the priesthood

But verses 5–7 are not about the priesthood. They are more a commentary on the king's rule.

> The Lord is at your right hand;
>   he will crush kings on the day of his wrath.
> He will judge the nations, heaping up the dead
>   and crushing the rulers of the whole earth.
> He will drink from a brook along the way,
>   and so he will lift his head high.

This is the domain of the king: ruling, confrontation, war. The enthronement of the priest-king—his session at the right hand of God—is therefore not the final setting but the prelude to world conquest.

Now Yahweh and his Messiah act as one. On the one hand,

> The Lord is at your right hand;
>> he will crush kings on the day of his wrath.
>
> He will judge the nations. (vv. 5–6)

On the other hand, he is this human figure who

> will drink from a brook along the way,
>> and so he will lift his head high. (v. 7)

Here is God bringing about conquest but somehow doing it through this human figure who takes a drink along the way.

Do you know what the closest New Testament language to this passage is? Revelation, especially chapter 19. For here you have moved from Hebrews and Melchizedek to the apocalypse and destruction.

> I saw heaven standing open and there before me was a white horse, whose rider is called Faithful and True. With justice he judges and wages war. His eyes are like blazing fire, and on his head are many crowns. He has a name written on him that no one knows but he himself. He is dressed in a robe dipped in blood, and his name is the Word of God. The armies of heaven were following him, riding on white horses and dressed in fine linen, white and clean. Coming out of his mouth is a sharp sword with which to strike down the nations. "He will rule them with an iron scepter." He treads the winepress of the fury of the wrath of God Almighty. On his robe and on his thigh he has this name written:
>
> KING OF KINGS AND LORD OF LORDS. (Rev. 19:11–16)

We have moved from the Melchizedekian vision of a priest in Hebrews to ultimate consummation in conquest and judgment.

But that makes Psalm 110:4 (the second oracle) all the stranger because not only does this psalm mingle priest and king, but even after introducing the priest—which seems strange enough—it does not comment on it.

WHAT IS DAVID THINKING?

So what is going on in David's head? What is he thinking about? I've thought about that one for a long time, and for a long time I think I got it wrong.

Modes of Inspiration

Inspiration in the Bible is by many modes. Sometimes it's by direct dictation. For example, God gives the words to Jeremiah; Jeremiah dictates them to Baruch; Baruch writes them down. That's why when the enemies come along and destroy the scroll that Baruch has written, the reader is supposed to laugh. The content in the scroll, after all, came from God. Do you really think God has forgotten it? Baruch might not be able to reproduce it, and Jeremiah may have forgotten a few lines here and there. But *God* dictated it. God's memory disks can never be wiped clean. So when the enemy destroys the scroll, God simply gives the words again to Jeremiah, who again dictates them to Baruch, who again writes them down. The only person who comes out somewhat disadvantaged on this one is Baruch because he has to write it all down again. But God is not going to forget the words of God.

Here, then, is inspiration by direct dictation.

Sometimes inspiration is by vision and word that the human agent himself does not even understand. Daniel, for example, asks what one of his visions means, and God essentially says, "Frankly, Daniel, it's none of your business. Seal up the book. It'll get sorted out later." Daniel is a transcriber, a witness, but he doesn't understand what he says, and the text says so.

Consider another mode of inspiration. You are not supposed to think of David coming in one night from a long session with his court counselors and saying, "Phew. Time to go to bed. This has been a tough day." So he stretches out, and then a voice says to him, "Not yet, David. I've got a psalm for you to write. Take out your quill pen." And David takes out his quill pen.

"All ready, David?"

"Ready."

"The Lord . . ."

"T-h-e L-o-r-d . . ."

". . . is my shepherd."

". . . i-s m-y s-h-e-p-h-e-r-d."

"I shall not want."

"I s-h-a-l-l n-o-t w-a-n-t."

There's no way that David wrote Psalm 23 that way. He wrote out of the fullness of his heart and the richness of his own experience. He wrote out of the overflow of creativity and his knowledge of the living God and his own background in the shepherd fields around Bethlehem. But borne along by the Spirit of God, so superintended by God's sovereignty, the words that came out are simultaneously David's words and the words of God.

That's another mode of inspiration. And we could mention several others.

So what is going on here in Psalm 110? Was David writing down these words because they were given by God, even though he himself did not understand them? If so, perhaps he was thinking, "I don't have a clue what verse 4 means, but it's going down." That's possible; after all, that is what Daniel experienced. For a long time I thought that was the most plausible way of imagining what was going on in David's head as he wrote verse 4. I just couldn't figure out how to read verse 4 in such a way that David could actually be making sense of it. So I thought, "This can't be a Psalm 23 sort of experience. It must be more of a Daniel mode of inspiration." Of course, this passage is not in an apocalyptic framework, like Daniel. Still, for a long time I thought that this was one of those relatively rare places in the Bible where it seems the human author didn't have a clue about what was going on.

But I've changed my mind. I think David got this in very substantial measure out of his devotions. His devotions? Yes, of course. After all, Deuteronomy 17 says what the king is supposed to do when he comes to power:

> When he takes the throne of his kingdom, he is to write for him-
> self on a scroll a copy of this law, taken from that of the Levitical
> priests. It is to be with him, and he is to read it all the days of his
> life so that he may learn to revere the LORD his God and follow
> carefully all the words of this law and these decrees and not con-
> sider himself better than his fellow Israelites and turn from the
> law to the right or to the left. (Deut. 17:18–20)

The king was supposed to copy out the book of the law and make
a nice clean copy. (There were no photocopy machines in those
days.) That clean copy was supposed to be his reading copy, which
he was then to read every day for the rest of his life so that he
would "not turn from the law to the right or to the left" but know
the Lord his God, please him, and not think of himself too highly.
Although many kings did not do this, David at his best was certainly doing this. Some of the kings were probably semi-literate,
but David was the sweet psalmist of Israel. He had a decent educa-
tion behind him. So doubtless David was having his devotions out
of the Word of God.

Now put yourself in David's place. He begins his reign in He-
bron in the south, ruling over the southern two tribes. After seven
years, he captures Jerusalem and becomes king over the twelve
tribes. So he moves to *Jerusalem*. Second Samuel 6 says that once
he is in Jerusalem, the tabernacle is moved to Jerusalem—and then
2 Samuel 7 establishes the Davidic dynasty. Do you hear that con-
catenation of things? The tabernacle, and thus the entire priestly
system, is in Jerusalem—for the first time in the same place as the
king: Jerusalem, the city of the king, the city of the high priest.

So now imagine David having his devotions, and one day he
comes to Genesis 14.

Genesis 14

Melchizedek first appears in Genesis 14. Let me remind you of
the context. There were four "kings." By "kings," you are not supposed to think of Charles III but instead something like a small-

town mayor. A lot of so-called "cities" in the ancient world had only 5,000 people; a big one was 10,000 or 15,000. Only the really big ones got to 200,000. So these are small-town mayors. They are "kings" of small communities. They are the commanders of little "armies" that are, in effect, raiding parties. Four of these get together under Kedorlaomer, and together they go on raids, gradually extending their reach. Eventually, they move farther south until they come into the area where Abram lives, and they attack the king of Sodom.

Sodom is allied with Gomorrah and three others, so now there are five kings against the four attacking kings. There is a nasty battle, and the four kings under Kedorlaomer win. They steal the women and children and cattle, kill as many of the men as possible, and take off toward the north.

"A man who had escaped came and reported this to Abram the Hebrew. Now Abram was living near the great trees of Mamre the Amorite, a brother of Eshkol and Aner, all of whom were allied with Abram" (Gen. 14:13). So now Abram and these other three allies go after the raiding party.

> When Abram heard that his relative had been taken captive, he called out the 318 trained men born in his household and went in pursuit as far as Dan. During the night Abram divided his men to attack them and he routed them, pursuing them as far as Hobah, north of Damascus. He recovered all the goods and brought back his relative Lot and his possessions, together with the women and the other people. (vv. 14–16)

"Trained men" does not mean that they are trained with rocket-propelled grenades or the latest in martial arts. I have a son who is a Marine trained in the martial arts and in I don't know how many weapons. I punched him in the shoulder a few years ago, and he put his big arm around me and said, rather kindly, "Dad, do you have any idea how many ways I could kill you with my bare hands?" I don't punch him in the shoulder anymore. The "trained men" in Genesis 14:14 are not trained in *that* sense. They are fit. They can do some stick fighting, maybe have the odd sword and many knives. But they take off after the four attacking kings, increasing their own numbers with whatever men come from the other three allies. They pursue the others "as far as Dan." That is something like 120–130 miles to the north, all on foot. They attack the enemies during the night and pursue them north of Damascus—an additional sixty miles or so north. That's the way a lot of those fights went. It's not that they drew battle lines like in World War I and lobbed howitzer shells at each other. There would be a big clash, and when one side started losing, they'd start to run. The other side would then chase them.

As Abram's group chases the fleeing raiding party, they pick up stolen people and goods that the raiding party is leaving behind. They keep pursuing the enemy until they're really not a threat anymore and the pursuers have collected all that they're going to collect. And then they start the long trek back.

> After Abram returned from defeating Kedorlaomer and the kings allied with him, the king of Sodom came out to meet him in the Valley of Shaveh (that is, the King's Valley). . . .
>   The king of Sodom said to Abram, "Give me the people and keep the goods for yourself." (vv. 17, 21)

The king of Sodom is not being generous here; he's merely following the custom of the day: that is, the reward for these mercenary groups would be the booty. They would return the stolen people and keep the stolen booty. Abram has every right to keep the booty.

> But Abram said to the king of Sodom, "With raised hand I have sworn an oath to the LORD, God Most High, Creator of heaven and earth, that I will accept nothing belonging to you, not even a thread or the strap of a sandal, so that you will never be able to say, 'I made Abram rich.' I will accept nothing but what my men have eaten and the share that belongs to the men who went with

me—to Aner, Eshkol and Mamre. Let them have their share."
(vv. 22–24)

If you skip verses 18–20, the account is entirely coherent. We
don't need those verses to make sense of the narrative. Just as the
mention of Melchizedek in Psalm 110 seems anomalous (What's
it doing there?), the mention of Melchizedek in Genesis 14:18–20
is anomalous (What's it doing here?). But not only is it there; it
actually breaks up the account of the interchange between Sodom
and Abram.

> Then Melchizedek king of Salem brought out bread and wine.
> He was priest of God Most High, and he blessed Abram, saying,
>
>> "Blessed be Abram by God Most High,
>>   Creator of heaven and earth.
>> And praise be to God Most High,
>>   who delivered your enemies into your hand."
>
> Then Abram gave him a tenth of everything. (vv. 18–20)

Now what should we learn from this? From the immediate context, Melchizedek clearly is a foil to Sodom. Abraham won't have
anything to do with Sodom; he doesn't want anything from Sodom
and won't give anything to him. There is a coldness between Abram
and Sodom. Sodom represents the wickedness of the valley. But
Melchizedek is a man of another order. His name itself is significant (as names so often are in the Old Testament). It means, quite
literally, "king of righteousness." (The *Melch*-root means "king," and
zedek means "righteousness.") He is the king whose name means
"king of righteousness": Your Majesty, King of Righteousness.

At the same time, he rules over Salem (v. 18). He is the king
of Salem. In Hebrew, you work by the consonants: *s-l-m*. Those
are the same consonants as *shalom*. In one context *shalom* can
mean simply "hi." But more richly, *shalom* refers to well-being—
well-being with God, well-being with human beings, well-being in

the richest sense of human flourishing. But undoubtedly this is the town of Salem. There were many towns called Salem in the ancient Near East; it was a pretty common name. The chances are very high, however, that since this is the area in which Abram is living at the time, the Salem in question refers to Jeru*salem*. Apparently, Melchizedek is king of Jerusalem, though we cannot be certain.

Salem means "peace." So Melchizedek is king of a town called Peace, while his name means "king of righteousness."

He brings out "bread and wine." This is the only detail in these three verses that the New Testament does not pick up. The New Testament does not find, for example, eucharistic symbolism here. Bread was a staple of the time, and wine was a common table drink (it was cut with water between three parts to one and ten parts to one). These poor chaps are famished; they're hungry and thirsty after their long trek back. Melchizedek meets them with huge quantities of supplies so that he is able to provide food and nourishment for these troops who have returned with the booty.

"He was priest of God Most High." When Abram speaks of God, he says, "With raised hand I have sworn an oath to the LORD [the covenant name for God], God Most High, Creator of heaven and earth" (v. 22). "God Most High" is a title for God used in connection with both Abram and Melchizedek, but another expression Abram uses ("the LORD [the covenant name for God]") is not associated with Melchizedek.

"He blessed Abram, saying, 'Blessed be Abram by God Most High, Creator of heaven and earth,'" which is exactly what Abram picks up when he speaks about God in verse 22.

Melchizedek continues, "And praise be to God Most High, who delivered your enemies into your hand." Abraham does not succeed, in the last analysis, because of his military prowess and the fitness of his 318 men. This is the work of God.

"Then Abram gave him a tenth of everything."

That's all the text says. But if you're a good reader, you have to start scratching your head and saying, "Okay, restricting ourselves to this text in Genesis, what's going on here? This is really strange. It breaks up the account. What are verses 18–20 contributing?" Indeed, this passage in Genesis is strange for another reason. In Genesis, everybody who is anybody is connected genealogically to other people. For example, read Genesis 5:

> When Adam had lived 130 years, he had a son in his own like-ness, in his own image; and he named him Seth. After Seth was born, Adam lived 800 years and had other sons and daughters. Altogether, Adam lived a total of 930 years, and then he died.
> When Seth had lived 105 years, he became the father of Enosh. After he became the father of Enosh, Seth lived 807 years and had other sons and daughters. Altogether, Seth lived a total of 912 years, and then he died. (Gen. 5:3–8)

Or alternatively, Genesis identifies people as "the son of" specific people.

But Melchizedek pops up, disappears, and there's no mention of a mommy or a daddy, and no genealogy. There are a few others in the book of Genesis without any mention of their genealogy, but at least they have the decency not to be important so that they don't raise any questions. But Melchizedek is so important that Abram actually pays him a tithe and receives a blessing from him. Abram himself—wealthy farmer and impressive figure that he is—receives a blessing from Melchizedek. Abram recognizes him as his superior.

Two Historic Interpretations of Melchizedek

So what is going on? In the history of the church, there have been two explanations for the figure of Melchizedek.

One is that Melchizedek is a pre-incarnate visitation of Jesus. That is, before Jesus becomes the God-man Jesus of Nazareth, the eternal Son appears in bodily form—an incarnation before the in-carnation. On this view, the eternal Son of God presents himself explicitly in human form in this Old Testament passage.

Many Christians think that that is what's going on here. If you hold that view, I will not attack it. In fact, nothing in my argument in the rest of this address depends on saying that this view is wrong. But I think it is wrong.

For a start, there is no hint that Melchizedek is a divine figure. Interestingly, Melchizedek does not use the name Yahweh. More importantly, why should we think that Abram was the only person in the entire ancient Near East who believed that there is only one God? We are not that far removed from Babel and the judgment of the flood. There must be some public memory here. Clearly there were many pagan kings around. But why shouldn't there be a king or two who acknowledged God Most High, Creator of heaven and earth? In that case, Abram may well have found in him a rather sympathetic figure. He may have become more intimately tied with him than he was with Mamre, Eshkol, and Aner. So when Abram receives some supplies from Melchizedek, Abram pays him due homage.

The passage remains strange because it says so little about this Melchizedek. But there are two other passages that make me think Melchizedek is unlikely to be a pre-incarnate presentation of Jesus (although we will see that he points to Jesus). One is found in Psalm 110; the other is found in Hebrews 7, and we'll consider it in a moment. For now, focus again on Psalm 110. If Genesis 14:18–20 really does report an incarnation of the second person of the Godhead, then Psalm 110:4 is almost incomprehensible.

> The Lord has sworn
>   and will not change his mind:
> "You are a priest forever,
>   *in the order of* Melchizedek."

Why does Psalm 110 say, "*in the order of* Melchizedek"? Why not say that "the Lord" *is* Melchizedek? Why not say, "You are a priest forever. You are indeed Melchizedek"? That would solve the problem. But instead he is a priest *in the order of* Melchizedek. Melchizedek is a model.

So what is going on in David's head? Don't forget: Just a few years earlier, David succeeded Saul, and he knows that Saul was killed and his line of succession destroyed because he had tried to be a priest-king. David is not going to make that mistake. So now David is having his devotions, and he reads Genesis 14 and discovers that there is a remarkable priest-king after all. There can't be anything intrinsically wicked about being a priest-king because even Abram recognized Melchizedek as the priest-king, paid him homage, and received blessings from him. David knows that he can't be a priest-king, but there can't be anything *intrinsically* wicked about it. David knows that Abraham lived about 2000 BC (not that he'd use that number or "BC" in those days) and that the law came about five hundred years in between Abraham and David. The law established the principle, "You cannot simultaneously be priest and king. The prohibition is absolute." But that law was not around, of course, when Abraham was alive, even if that law is now absolute in David's day. But David can't help thinking, as he's having his devotions, that maybe someday we'll have a priest-king again because Melchizedek is an enigmatic figure *superior to Abraham*—Abraham the progenitor of the entire covenantal race—who is priest-king. Melchizedek is the priest-king of God Most High, Creator of heaven and earth.

And by whatever insight beyond that, the Holy Spirit carries David along, and David picks up his pen and writes,

> The LORD has sworn
>   and will not change his mind:
> "You are a priest forever,
>   *in the order of* Melchizedek."

Psalm 110 is about a priest-king. His priesthood is not in the order of Levi, for that would be against the law. When Saul flouted that law, he was punished. And yet, a priest, a priest-king in the order of Melchizedek? That, surely, is possible. That is what Psalm 110 announces.

Psalm 110 hangs there for another thousand years. It just hangs there, waiting.

HEBREWS 7

Melchizedek is mentioned elsewhere in Hebrews, but we will focus on Hebrews 7. The book of Hebrews is often said to distort the Old Testament when it quotes it; allegedly, it twists things around and gets them wrong. But listen carefully to what the text says, and you discover that the writer is engaged in serious exegesis. He is reading what is there in the text: "This Melchizedek was king of Salem and priest of God Most High. He met Abraham returning from the defeat of the kings and blessed him, and Abraham gave him a tenth of everything" (Heb. 7:1–2a). That summarizes Genesis 14. Now the exegesis comes. The author of Hebrews thinks that the meaning of the Hebrew name Melchizedek is theologically significant:

> First, the name Melchizedek means "king of righteousness"; then also, "king of Salem" means "king of peace." Without father or mother [so far as the text goes], without genealogy [that's the point], without beginning of days or end of life [so far as the text goes], resembling the Son of God, he remains a priest forever. (Heb. 7:2b–3)

If Melchizedek really *is* "the Son of God," then the reason "he remains a priest forever" is that he *is* the eternal son of God. But the author of Hebrews is saying something different. Melchizedek, he asserts, resembles the Son of God; he is *like* the Son of God. This conclusion he grounds in the observation that there is theological weight *in what is left out*: there is no mention of mother or father or genealogy or death. Of course, arguments from silence can be very weak. But an argument from silence is very strong if you are expecting noise. Read Sherlock Holmes's "The Dog That Barked in the Night." The point is that the dog *didn't* bark in the night. This dog always barked when there was a stranger around. Somebody came and did something in the house, and the dog didn't bark. The silence was significant because the dog always barked at strangers. Therefore, it had to be someone who wasn't a stranger to the dog.

Whether or not there is a genealogy is insignificant in some contexts. But if everyone who is significant in the book of Genesis does have a genealogy, it's significant when suddenly someone is introduced who *doesn't* have a genealogy. You must draw some inferences. The author of Hebrews is saying, "As God has given us this account, there is weight to the fact that Melchizedek is not said to have a father or mother—no genealogy. As far as the record goes, it doesn't list his birth or death." Earlier in Genesis, there are lots of beginnings and deaths. But Melchizedek simply shows up and disappears. Thus, Melchizedek is *like* an eternal priest who lives forever.

So I don't think it's necessary to argue that Melchizedek is a pre-incarnate appearance of the eternal Son. Instead, this is an example of what we often see in the Old Testament: patterns, institutions, and people put in place with all kinds of symbol-laden structures around them that point forward until you come to the reality itself.

Notice further the exegesis of Hebrews:

> Just think how great he was: Even the patriarch Abraham gave him a tenth of the plunder! Now the law [i.e., the law of Moses, which comes more than half a millennium *after* Abraham] requires the descendants of Levi who become priests to collect a tenth from the people—that is, from their fellow Israelites—even though they also are descended from Abraham. [I.e., the law authorized the Levites, the ultimate grandchildren of Abraham, to collect tithes.] This man, however, did not trace his descent from Levi, yet he collected a tenth from Abraham and blessed him who had the promises. And without doubt the lesser is blessed by the greater. (Heb. 7:4–7)

All of this argumentation shows just how important Melchizedek is. All of the argument is straightforward exegesis.

Then we come to a big jump. When we start talking about how to preach Christ from the Old Testament, one of the ways into that discussion is to examine how the New Testament quotes the Old. So you start from the back end and see how the New Testament quotes the Old. You discover that it does so in a huge diversity of ways: sometimes by analogy, sometimes by direct prediction, sometimes in word-association games, sometimes appealing to common theological themes, sometimes by something we call typology. With typology, there is a pattern: an institution or person, place, thing gets repeated and repeated and ratcheted up until you expect there to be something bigger that brings the pattern to a climax.

This typology introduces an additional factor. That factor shows up half a dozen times in the Bible and is hinted at in other places. But this way of quoting the Old Testament is spectacularly insightful. I'm going to get at this one through the side door.

If you were a conservative first-century Jew and you were asked, "How do you please God?" how would you answer? You would answer, I think, by saying, "By obeying the law."

"How did Daniel please God?"

"He obeyed the law."

"How did David please God?"

"He obeyed the law."

"How did Isaiah please God?"

"He obeyed the law."

"How did Abraham please God?"

"He obeyed the law."

"Oh—wait a minute. Abraham didn't have the law. He lived before the law.

"But the text says, 'Abraham obeyed me and did everything I required of him, keeping my commands, my decrees and my instructions' (Gen. 26:5). He must have had a private revelation of the law."

"How did Enoch please God?"

"He obeyed the law."

"Wait a minute. Enoch was only seventh from Adam. He didn't have the law. Neither Abraham nor Moses even existed yet. That's desperately anachronistic."

"Yes, but the text says, 'Enoch walked faithfully with God' (Gen. 5:24). That is common language after the giving of the law for obeying the law. So undoubtedly for Enoch to obey God, he had to obey the law. He too must have been given a private revelation of the law, which he then kept."

Now what are you doing by this kind of reading of the Old Testament? You are elevating the law to be the hermeneutical control over the entire text. So you have taken away the steps of progress in history, and all you have instead is the law controlling how you read the entire narrative.

Then you come to the New Testament writers. Paul almost certainly would have interpreted the Old Testament account the way I have just described *before he became a Christian*. But now he is a Christian. And when Paul becomes a Christian, he sees that when he reads the Old Testament, *sequence* is important. Read Galatians 3: God gave his promise to Abraham *before* he gave the law, and the law can't annul the promise. Abraham was justified by faith *before* the giving of the law. That is a grounding that is established before the law comes. That is a *sequential* reading of the Old Testament. First-century conservative Palestinian Jews didn't read the text that way. But the *sequence* is really important for Paul to authorize that the gospel saves people by faith.

Now you see something of the same sort here in Hebrews 7. Look at the argument: "If perfection could have been attained through the Levitical priesthood [that came through the law] . . . why was there still need for another priest to come, one in the order of Melchizedek, not in the order of Aaron?" (Heb. 7:11). If the ultimate priesthood was the Levitical priesthood and the law of Moses was final, then why on earth is David saying what he says in Psalm 110 centuries after the law was given? By announcing a priest in the order of Melchizedek, David implicitly says that the Levitical priesthood somehow isn't good enough. It must be eclipsed. So one thousand years before Jesus comes, already David's psalm says, in effect, "We must have more than a Levitical priesthood. It's not enough." David implicitly announces the need for a priesthood that outstrips the Levitical priesthood prescribed by the law of Moses.

Then watch how the argument goes: "For when the priesthood is changed, the law must be changed also" (Heb. 7:12). Go back to that little parenthetical bit that I let out in verse 11: "If perfection could have been attained through the Levitical priesthood—*and indeed the law given to the people established that priesthood*—why was there still need for another priest to come, one in the order of Melchizedek, not in the order of Aaron?" The law and the priesthood are so tied together (one establishes the other) that if you take one away, then the other one is gone too.

Sometimes we think of the law as divided into three categories: moral, civil, and ceremonial. That's a common breakdown, and it has many kinds of utilitarian value. As a result, however, we tend to say, "The civil law is not all that important, and the ceremonial law is not all that important. The moral law is the really important thing." The result is that we love to meditate on Exodus 20 because it has the Ten Commandments, and then we sort of skim through Leviticus without much thought because so much of it is devoted to ceremonial law—and ceremonial law is what establishes the Levitical priesthood. But Hebrews 7 says that if you pull that priesthood out, then you change the entire law covenant. The entire law covenant is in principle obsolete as soon as you start announcing that the Levitical priesthood is obsolete. If one is obsolete, so is the other.

The entire argument is grounded in sequence:

1. Abraham encounters this vague figure Melchizedek. This happens before God gives the law. Melchizedek is a priest-king.
2. More than half a millennium later, the law says the same person cannot be both priest and king.

3. Centuries later, David says that there will be a priest-king in the order of Melchizedek. Thus, David makes the law, in principle, obsolete. This announces a new covenant in principle one thousand years before the coming of Jesus.

4. The author of Hebrews says that we now have a priest-king— not from the tribe of Levi (that would be illegitimate) but from the tribe of Judah. Thus, the entire law covenant is in some sense obsolete.

"He of whom these things are said belonged to a different tribe, and no one from that tribe has ever served at the altar" (Heb. 7:13). That's Jesus, who came from the tribe of Judah. The next verses explain:

> For it is clear that our Lord descended from Judah, and in regard to that tribe Moses said nothing about priests. And what we have said is even more clear if another priest like Melchizedek appears, one who has become a priest not on the basis of a regulation as to his ancestry but on the basis of the power of an indestructible life. (vv. 14–16)

"A regulation as to his ancestry"—that's what the *Levites* enjoyed. They had to have the right mother and father; they had to go back through Zadok all the way to Aaron; this was a regulation as to their ancestry.

But there is no ancestry to the historical figure Melchizedek. And Jesus's ancestry according to the flesh is—Joseph? While Jesus is the son of Mary, his ultimate ancestry is grounded in the God of eternity: without father, without mother.

For it is declared,

> "You are a priest forever,
> in the order of Melchizedek." (v. 17)

This cites Psalm 110. Hebrews continues:

> The former regulation [i.e., the regulation about Levitical priests] is set aside because it was weak and useless (for the law

made nothing perfect), and a better hope is introduced, by which we draw near to God.

And it was not without an oath! Others became priests without any oath [i.e., priests in the Levitical system did not take oaths when they became priests], but he became a priest with an oath when God said to him:

> "The LORD has sworn
> and will not change his mind:
> 'You are a priest forever.'"

Because of this oath, Jesus has become the guarantor of a better covenant. (Heb. 7:18–22)

Then the author of Hebrews spells out pastoral implications:

> Now there have been many of those priests, since death prevented them from continuing in office; but because Jesus lives forever, he has a permanent priesthood. Therefore he is able to save completely those who come to God through him, because he always lives to intercede for them. (vv. 23–25)

CONCLUSION

I have spent an undue amount of time explaining how these passages work because I want you to see that the New Testament authors are reading the Old Testament carefully. The New Testament authors observe the historical sequence in order to draw inferences that cannot easily be refuted. If you announce the coming of a priest-king (a) after God himself has said in his law covenant that there must not be a priest-king and (b) on the basis of a figure who shows up before that law covenant, then you are saying that the law covenant that forbids a priest-king is temporary and obsolete.

That means that the One we are looking for is not only the Davidic Messiah, the kingly ruler. He is also the priest. We must learn to see, understand, admire, and follow the traces of the wisdom of God in putting together the whole canon in these long trajectories that bring us along axis after axis to Jesus.

I just followed *one* axis that appears in only three passages. But you can follow similar trajectories regarding the temple, Passover, Yom Kippur, Sabbath and rest, the Day of Jubilee, the twelve tribes, the city of Jerusalem, and much more. You can track out all of these lines. Work hard at understanding how the New Testament handles the Old Testament, and you will learn how to preach the Old Testament, because these New Testament passages show the trajectories that God himself has put in place. And they point forward and bring us to Jesus. I say this to give you confidence to read the Word of God carefully, to listen to it, probe it, and discover for yourself how the New Testament writers themselves read the Old Testament. Then go and do likewise.

I want to end with one more observation. I have focused a disproportionate amount of time on the mechanics of these texts, how they are tied together. But you must see the theological payoff. We have a Savior who not only is the *king*—the promised king, who rules over our lives, who confronts the enemies of God, and who consummates all things—but also is the promised priest. Yes, Jesus is the king and conqueror, and we must bow in submission to his kingdom. But he is also the *priest* in the order of Melchizedek.

If Jesus is just a king, then we live in terror. But he is also the priest. He is the perfect Mediator between God and human beings because he is God and a human being. He exactly takes up all the functions and purposes of the Old Testament priests, but he outstrips them in one huge particular: he never sinned. The author of Hebrews goes on to talk about that. That is why Jesus is an even *better* high priest than they were.

> Such a high priest truly meets our need—one who is holy, blameless, pure, set apart from sinners, exalted above the heavens. Unlike the other high priests, he does not need to offer sacrifices day after day, first for his own sins, and then for the sins of the people. He sacrificed for their sins once for all when he offered himself. For the law appoints as high priests men in all their

weakness; but the oath, which came after the law, appointed the Son, who has been made perfect forever. (Heb. 7:26–28)

Moreover, they offered inferior sacrifices. Does the blood of a bull and goat actually have some sort of intrinsic moral value? Does that make sense? The bullock is not saying, "Here's my throat. Go ahead and slit it. I'm dying for you." In that sense, it is a morally useless sacrifice. What does it mean to take the blood of a goat and substitute it for the blood of a human being? It doesn't make sense. It is pointing forward to something else: the Lamb of God.

Wonderful, merciful Savior,
Precious Redeemer and Friend,
Who would have thought that a lamb
Could ransom the souls of men?[3]

And what a Lamb this One is. He is the priest, and he turns out to be the sacrifice. And he is the temple, the place where human beings meet the holy God. He is the temple, priest, and lamb, and his body is the veil. Again and again he takes all these strands to himself. We come to the New Testament text, and our eyes see how the Old Testament patterns in God's perfect wisdom have anticipated all this. We see the fulfillment, and we bow and worship.

God knows that I need a king to subdue me and to bring in the consummation. I need a priest to offer up himself as the supreme sacrifice, or I am undone. I need a perfect priest—one of our kind, a human being, who is nevertheless one with God, without mother and without father (in the most ultimate sense), with everlasting days.

This is the Jesus of the gospel we proclaim.

Before the throne of God above,
I have a strong and perfect plea,
A great high priest whose name is love,
Who ever lives and pleads for me.[4]

---

[3] "Wonderful, Merciful Savior," Dawn Rodgers and Eric Wyse, copyright © 1989 Word Music.
[4] Charitie Lees Smith, "The Advocate," 1863.

Oh, Lord God, we do not want to make the reading of the Old Testament a merely cerebral exercise, but we do want to understand what your Word says, that we may draw near in confidence to Christ Jesus, our beloved king, our priest, made for us everything we need, such that we find full confidence in him. Open our eyes that we may see, and in seeing believe, and in believing obey; for Jesus's sake. Amen.

CONTRIBUTORS

Alistair Begg is Senior Pastor of Parkside Church near Cleveland, Ohio.

Mike Bullmore is Senior Pastor of Crossway Community Church in Bristol, Wisconsin.

D. A. Carson is Research Professor of New Testament at Trinity Evangelical Divinity School.

Matt Chandler is Lead Pastor of The Village Church in the Dallas metroplex.

Tim Keller is Senior Pastor of Redeemer Presbyterian Church in New York City.

James MacDonald is Senior Pastor of Harvest Bible Chapel in the greater Chicago area.

Conrad Mbewe is Pastor of Kabwata Baptist Church in Lusaka, Zambia.

R. Albert Mohler Jr. is President of The Southern Baptist Theological Seminary.

GENERAL INDEX

SCRIPTURE INDEX

It's time to reclaim the core of our beliefs...

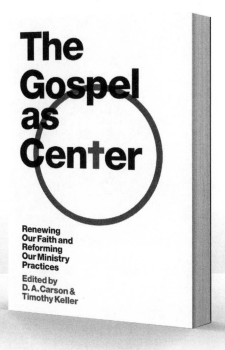

Important aspects of Christianity are in danger of being lost as relativism takes root in our churches today. What was historically agreed upon is now readily questioned and the very essentials of the Christian faith are in jeopardy.

In response, **D. A. Carson, Tim Keller, Kevin DeYoung,** and other influential leaders have created this volume to defend the traditional gospel and to strengthen the church.

The Gospel as Center will help you join in the movement and stand united under the conviction that what holds us together is worth fighting for.